Operation Success

OPERATION SUCCESS

by

QUENTIN REYNOLDS

and

WILFRID S. ROWE

DUELL, SLOAN AND PEARCE

New York

First Edition

Library of Congress Catalog Card No. 57-11066

May, 1970

PATTERNS OF SUCCESS

FROM THE

QUENTIN REYNOLDS

TELEVISION PROGRAM

"OPERATION SUCCESS"

PRODUCED BY

R. JASON PHILLIPS

AUTHOR'S NOTE

THIS BOOK REPRESENTS AN HONEST EFFORT TO CONVEY AN IMpression of successful men and organizations. The men and their organizations are interlocked. Where possible, the outstanding ingredients of the individual's success have been isolated and named. Many of the ingredients have trite names: honesty, faith, the will to serve, dynamic drive. It may be felt that the positive ingredients appear too often or too clearly, but no attempt has been made to seek out failings in the men presented here. We rate our golfers by their playing ability, not by the practice swings. We rate our ball players by their hits, not their misses. The same thing is done here for the men who keep the wheels of our economy turning.

In some cases, it is impossible to isolate the ingredients that make the successful man; instead, incidents and quotations attempt to reveal the way a man tackles a problem, the way he thinks or feels.

There is not a person in these pages who was not most gracious with time and encouragement.

FOREWORD

ABOUT THREE YEARS AGO A BRIGHT YOUNG TELEVISION PRODUCER named Jason Phillips came up with what the advertising boys on Madison Avenue call a "gimmick." A "gimmick" in the trade is a new idea, or formula, or a new way of presenting an old idea.

Phillips wanted to do a TV show to be called "Operation Success," which would feature men and women who had hit the jackpot in our world of free enterprise. He would present only those, however, whose stories were interesting. His plan called for someone like myself to interview each of these before a camera. That interview would be part of the television show, and the rest would be a film made in the factory or enterprise headed by our guest. I was dubious about the venture. The Horatio Alger books stopped selling long ago, and this looked to be a kind of road-company Alger. I felt that most successful businessmen would tell just about the same story. Repetition would soon impel viewers either to doze or hurriedly to turn their dials to another station.

I was 100 per cent wrong. Our program has been running for nearly three years. I have interviewed some three hundred men and women and haven't heard the same story twice.

I had previously thought that there was some basic pattern which, if followed, would bring a man to the top of his profession. That just isn't true. By now I know that there are no rules, no set guideposts for a man to follow to success. Some of our guests were born in abject poverty; some were sons of wealthy parents; the majority were born of parents in the middle-income brackets. Some made their marks early in life

(there are 1200 members of the Young Presidents' Organization, composed of men who achieved the presidency of a concern before the age of forty). Some didn't make it until late in
life. Some of our guests were solemn, quiet men; others were
gay, laughing characters. Some had never graduated from elementary school; some were brilliant scientists with doctor's
degrees. Some were politically conservative; others were liberal.
These successful men and women did not conform to any pattern; each was an individual *different* from the others.

Sometimes, in the most unexpected places, a person would
say to me, "By the way, *how* did Mr. So-and-so make a success
of his business?" Others on the "Operation Success" staff were
asked the same question. We began looking, subconsciously at
first, for the spark in each of our guests that had moved him to
the head of the class.

One day, after interviews were finished and "in the can" as
the cameraman says, several of us started comparing answers to
the recurring question. Before we were aware of all the twists
and turns the conversation had taken, we were discussing the
"how" of success in terms of a book. To me it seemed that a
book, dealing with individuals at greater length than I could
during an interview for television, would be a natural outgrowth of the "Operation Success" program. Jason Phillips
grew so enthusiastic he infected me with the idea. Bill Rowe—he
has written the narrative scripts for the TV show for more than
two and a half years—grew as warm as Phillips about the idea.

There is a great difference between the birth of an idea and
the birth of a book. The book was born slowly; despite that,
we wish there were more stories in it. There are other wonderful success stories to be told by our program guests, but the
time came when the publisher had to cry halt.

The result? It isn't a hard-and-fast rule book or set of guideposts pointing a single, straight road to success. As I said before,
no two people told the same story. Well, if it isn't a rule book,
you may ask, what is it? I would answer that question this way:

no two of us are made of identical mental building blocks. We can use certain ideas that fit our philosophy and our work habits. Others simply won't fit and we reject them. So a rule book can be written for only a limited audience, and this book is for everyone interested in learning how others have achieved success. If in some of the stories there is nothing that you can apply to your own life and career, you'll find ideas in the others that you can use.

Adopt or adapt whatever you can. After all, a number of successful persons have climbed the ladder because of a single abiding idea. Let me close this foreword the way I close each "Operation Success" program, and wish you "continued success in whatever you do."

QUENTIN REYNOLDS

CONTENTS

Operation Success

1. FIRED—TO SUCCESS

Eugene T. Turney, Jr., of North Shore Nameplate

In 1956, THE BIMINI WHITE MARLIN TROPHY WAS RETURNED to the United States by a short, tough Irish-American who fishes for the big ones the way he works and plays. He plays earnestly; he works sincerely; he fishes in the same manner.

Today the Bimini Trophy is in Eugene T. Turney, Jr.'s, "den"—a larger, more quietly elaborate room than the word "den" implies—in his fourteen-room, white-pillared house located on a wide, shaded green acre in Bayside, Long Island. The same room has an electric organ that Gene Turney taught himself to play. "It's better than pills and cheaper than a doctor," Gene says. A baby grand in the opposite corner has beginners' music books marked for the instruction of his seven-year-old daughter, Suzy. Comfortable sofas and marble-topped coffee tables, a hi-fi record player, driftwood lamps, and potted plants fill the large room.

The largest sailfish ever caught—and Gene Turney caught it—hangs on one wall. Trophies and citations are in an orderless array beneath it. Turney is proud of them, but there is no ostentation, no great display—just as there is no ostentation concerning the electric organ. In the summer, Turney wanders in stripped to the waist and works the foot pedals with his feet in moccasins.

His business, North Shore Nameplate, Inc., is located about a mile away. Seeing the comfort of his home, its near location to his business, and knowing that he knocks off work to fish at Montauk Point, Bimini, or Miami, one could easily believe that Turney was born with a silver spoon in his mouth. The truth is considerably different.

Walk through North Shore Nameplate today, and you will see a humming business that was founded on the twin pillars of failure and impossibility. Not a very auspicious beginning. Now, linotypes click, offset presses whir, slitting and cutting machines add to the general sound of activity. The various machines—most of them adapted by Turney from their original purposes or, at least, from their specified production standards—produce wire markers and name plates.

Wire markers and name plates! To the ordinary citizen, either or both of those items probably sound like something that a person might use once in a lifetime. So you should know that both name plates and wire markers are used in abundance. In construction, in building electrical and electronic equipment, wires are identified with pressure-sensitive tape. The tape has a number printed on it—not once, but many times. A construction electrician or assembler of electrical equipment tears off a piece of tape and slaps it around a wire. It simplifies connection work.

What could be simpler than a piece of tape with "2-2-2-2-2-2" printed on it? The answer is, a lot of things are simpler to make, as Gene Turney found out the hard way when the wire-marker manufacturing company that he and his wife, Margaret, had been representing since 1950 suddenly swung the ax. One day the Turney selling team had wire markers to offer in a fruitful market; the next day they had none. It was a bitter blow, but it wasn't the first that had been dealt to Turney—or the last.

The other item in the Turney team's selling kit was name plates. And you should know that name plates, like wire markers, are big business in the United States. Electrical and mechanical equipment, tools, cameras, and household appliances have from one to a hundred name plates. Some are simple oblongs of metal or foil that give the name of the manufacturer and the trade name of the article. Others have holes punched through their centers and say "ON" and "OFF," showing which way to throw a switch. Still others are more intricate, giving operating instructions. And the cream of the crop are printed with schematic diagrams that act as guides for repairmen fixing broken circuits in complex electronic equipment. Manufacturers buy name plates in great quantity and variety.

Turney has a sense of responsibility and values. His dogged feeling of responsibility toward customers had him in hot water more than once with the name-plate manufacturer he represented. And he represented that particular concern because they made foil, rather than metal, plates. There is a great saving in weight and in the time required to apply foil name plates, as compared to their metal counterparts. Gene and his wife knew how to sell the advantages of foil plates—and their ability brought them a good living. It was a better living than Gene had made when he ran the round-lot "Sell" wire at the Stock Exchange, for instance.

When he was a youngster ("Had a hell of a time getting through high school," Turney confided), he was an amateur radio operator. Licensed at the age of eleven, Gene became a radio officer on a banana boat when he was sixteen. Later he worked as a Wall Street telegraph operator and was on the floor of the Stock Exchange the day of the crash in 1929—which, for the operator of the "Sell" wire, was one of the longest days in recorded history.

Shortly thereafter, Gene and Peg, as he calls his wife, were operating a sign shop in Danbury, Connecticut. (Gene had applied gold leaf to the windows of a chain of cigar stores before shipping on the banana boat, but decided he didn't like it.) They would paint anything from the side of a building—both of them aloft on a scaffold—to a small card for a dress shop. The crash was still fresh in everyone's mind; a dollar was hard to get; the Turneys would letter anything, if the job meant money. Once they walked into a newly opened barbershop, attracted by its freshly applied gold-leaf lettering.

"How much did you pay for that lettering?" Gene asked.

"Thirty dollars," said the barber.

"Thirty dollars!" Gene exclaimed. "That's too much. I'll do it for twenty."

The barber knew a bargain when he saw one. He promptly razor-bladed the thirty-dollar gold-leaf sign off his window, and Gene did the job over again, collected his twenty—and beat it before the barber realized what had happened to him.

As with most people, the fortunes of the Turneys took a turn for the better as the years this side of '29 went by. Gene found time to indulge his passion for boating (he holds the coveted rank of JN—Junior Navigator—in the United States Power Squadron), pistol shooting, and, most of all, fishing. Game fishing. Marlin, barracuda, and sailfish hold particular appeal for this man of action. He has landed 102-pound marlin with thread rated at 20 pounds test. Seven stitches circle his right thumb where a barracuda nearly severed it after Gene had worked it close to the boat and knocked it over the head. That was probably the only misdirected blow he ever aimed in his life—whether he was going after fish or business.

Yes, the fortunes of the Turneys were better. Comfortable house, nice car, no question about sending their four children through college. They were no longer scrambling for a dollar as in the Danbury days, but they were not growing soft, either, and the future looked bright—until the day they were summarily cut off from their long-established source of wire markers. But a man who catches 100-pound marlin with a twenty-pound test line is a fighting sportsman—not likely to lie around and lick his wounds when the ax falls. That was certainly true of Turney.

He had never seen wire markers made. He merely knew that, to be able to meet the competition, you must have sheets of numbered tape in stock—about thirty different numbers to a sheet—with numbers ranging from 1 to 1,000. You must be able to sell a sheet for about a dime. The electrician must be able to peel the numbers off their fiber backing quickly and be able to apply them without effort.

"I found a small engineering company in the wrong end of Jersey that said they could build a machine to perform anything," is the way E. T. Turney, Jr., tells of his initial intrusion into the wire-marker field. "Twelve thousand dollars later we had a machine, all right, but nobody could run it, including the man who had built it.

"A few thousand dollars later the machine would run on Monday, but it wouldn't run on Tuesday. We played around with that for a couple of months, and finally found that the fiber we were using for backing the tape soaked up so much moisture out of the air that the 155-pound rolls we ran with no trouble on Monday weighed 168 pounds on Tuesday. It just swelled up and got too thick to run through the press.

"We licked that, and then we really started to pile up inventory. Have to have a big inventory, because you have to ship the day an order comes in or the business goes to somebody else. In the meantime, of course, we got into typography and printing problems, and I had to learn a lot about adhesives, too.

"We started shipping wire markers, and they were beautiful. That is, they were beautiful when they left the plant, but a day or two later you could rub the ink right off them with your pinky. So I had to learn something about printing inks. Then we started spraying a varnish finish on the tapes.

"Those varnished tapes were beauts, too. I still have a drawer full of them somewhere around the office. They're all pink. It seems that the varnish we used fought with the tape, and the varnish won. They all turned a gorgeous shade of pink—and nobody wanted pink wire markers. So we started all over again."

Fortunately, Turney had put aside a share of his earnings when his fortunes had improved. He doesn't like "outside money." It's hard to do business without it—but he still had a fairly well-assured income from the sale of foil name plates made by the second firm he represented. Then the name-plate manufacturer swung the ax.

Gene announced the severance to his wife by saying, "Well, Peg, now we're going to start making name plates." All the problems that arose in learning, from scratch, how to make wire markers were tripled when the Turneys set out to learn how to produce anodized-foil name plates. On the face of it, they were challenging an impossibility compounded several times over. First, anodizing foil that is only .003-inch thick is practically impossible. Yes, there was one firm that could do it, but they weren't publishing a handbook for upstart competitors to follow. Second, available machinery could not print the foil even if he did succeed in anodizing it, and specially built machinery would cost more than the Turneys could raise. Third, Gene demanded a degree of accuracy in the finished plates that he was assured could not be obtained. Fourth—and this is one of the principal stumbling blocks that land new business ventures in bankruptcy—neither Turney nor any of his workmen had any experience or know-how in the name-plate field. In other words, he couldn't do it. Sure, said Turney—just as the captain told me I couldn't land that barracuda with a twenty-pound line.

His education had stopped with high school, according to the records, but a man such as Gene Turney never ends his education. He teaches himself. Every scrap of experience is stored away for future reference. For instance, the hi-fi record player in his den is better than its highly regarded manufacturer made it. From his ham radio days, ship, and stock exchange experience, Gene had accumulated enough knowledge to tear out and improve the player's rectifier circuit and improve on the balance and arrangement of speakers. So, from his mental warehouse, he was able to put scraps and shreds of knowledge and experience together and, looking at a finished name plate, outline the various steps that it must go through from the time it was delivered as a piece of plain aluminum.

"First," said Gene, "I had to have an anodizing plant."

"Wouldn't it have been simpler to have your anodizing done outside?" he was asked.

"Sure—but if my anodizer went on strike or felt he had to give preference to an older customer, I could lose my shirt—and if I was going to lose my shirt, I wanted to do it all by myself."

Anodizing is the process by which a colored surface is put on metal. It requires close control of every factor. "We chucked out a bargeload of streaked plates before we discovered that the city of New York had decided to throw more chlorine into the water that day. Now we have an arrangement with the city; they tell us when they are going to change the chlorine content. Anything at all can make your anodizing process go haywire. ... You learn," he adds laconically.

At the time the anodizing plant was being rigged up (the acid bath ate up $8,000 worth of special screws at 40 cents apiece before that profit leak was stopped up), the basic minimum equipment for the name-plate factory and personnel to operate it were being assembled. The equipment, remember, had to be specially made, so Gene bought standard equipment and did everything but beat it with his bare fists to make it do special jobs. The big problem was to get into production at the earliest possible date. As Gene Turney saw it, every day that passed without finished name plates being produced was a day of potential profit that was lost forever. The problems involved are probably best explained by outlining the steps involved in producing name plates—the way Turney wanted them produced.

An artist—frequently working with an engineer—designs the name plate. He gives the name-plate company a drawing and any art work that will be part of the finished plate. The name-plate maker sets type, pulls reproduction proofs of it in the required sizes, then has one of his own artists paste the type in place—which may be as simple as it sounds on one job and in-

finitely time-consuming on the next. The paste-up goes in front
of an engraver's camera and a negative is made. If there are any
cross rules or fine lines in the art work, the focus must be extremely sharp, and that sharpness must be held through all
succeeding steps to produce a finished plate that does not blur
on fine type or where thin lines intersect. (To digress for a
moment, this single phase of production led President Turney
into a study of optics, then he improved his engraver's camera
just as he had stepped up the quality of his hi-fi player at home.)

If many copies of a small name plate are required, the original
negative is run through a "step-and-repeat" copying camera,
which automatically reproduces the negative over and over
again on a second negative. These cameras cost a prince's, if not
a king's, ransom. They are precision machines in every detail,
so that the repeated negatives on the completed sheets of printed
name plates are all in exact position to one another, so that there
will be no variation between one name plate and another.
(After "making do" with a hand-operated affair of his own
devising at the outset, Turney bought the best on the market—
and improved it to meet his personal standards for quality.)

The negative is held against a sensitized aluminum offset
printing plate, and strong arc lights burn the negative image
into the aluminum. The image is then "fixed," the plate is
washed, and is ready for the offset press. Here, again, adaptation of standard equipment to a special purpose was required.
The relatively small offset press that North Shore Nameplate,
Inc., required was built to print on paper, not metal foil.
Turney had to learn something about printing and the inner
workings of presses that, to a layman, seems unnecessarily
complicated for the apparently simple job of transferring ink
from a roller to a piece of paper, or, as in this case, foil.

The ink—much gummier than ordinary printing ink—is
coated with powder. Immediately after powdering, a strong
vacuum-cleaning arrangement removes *all* excess powder—that
is, all powder not covering ink. The ink and powder are fused

and baked under infrared lamps. The foil plate is then run through an acid bath which eats away all anodized finish that is not protected by the baked-on powder-in mixture. A second bath removes that protective coating, revealing the finished name plate.

A number of individual name plates are usually made on a single sheet of foil—which was the reason for installing the step-and-repeat machine. Next, the foil sheets pass through a special laminating machine which applies a pressure-sensitive adhesive backing and a protective fiber covering. "Special" is the kindest description possible; the machine in action resembles a Walt Disney version of a scarecrow dancing the tango.

The sheets are cut apart. If required, the corners of the individual name plates are rounded. The name plates are inspected and packed in vinyl plastic bags to keep them daisy fresh until used.

The user strips off the protective backing, presses the name plate in position, and it's there to stay. North Shore's "Therma Cal" name plates are applied with heat so that they will not peel off under continuous high temperatures. Turney's dabbling in adhesives led to the development of a spray-on adhesive (packed in an Aerosol bomb for easy application) that will hold a name plate to a crackle finish. His name plates can be applied to anything that will stand still—without drilling holes, inserting rivets, screws, or escutcheon pins. North Shore will produce name plates in combinations of several anodized colors. Turney's study of optics and the resulting sharp focus of his camera work have brought him unexpected business from platemakers who cannot match the sharp, high quality of the work done by the man who is not, essentially, a platemaker. His related equipment has led naturally to more and more frequent printing and direct-mail advertising jobs—and Gene is not essentially a printer or advertising man. "This business is crazy enough without becoming an advertising agency," Turney says, and he speaks from experience, having been an account executive and technical copy writer for an agency at one point in his career.

Gene hates neckties, so he doesn't wear them unless the occasion demands. On "demand" occasions, he wears a conservative four-in-hand, not pressing his informality to the point of Bohemianism. When you phone him at his office, you get through to him. "If somebody asks for me, I guess they want to speak to me." His telephone conversations are brief, clipped, to the point. When he works, he works in earnest, but if time permits, he will tell you about the overflow of trophies and stuffed prize-winning fish that decorate his office. If Gene Turney wanted to be a stuffed shirt, learning how to play the part would give him more trouble than learning how to make wire markers and name plates presented.

The man soaks up whatever experience tosses his way, and he files it mentally for future reference. Whether he is going after a big one off Montauk, or an order in Chicago, the matter at hand receives his full attention, and chances are high that he will land it. "Stick with a problem long enough," he says, "and you'll fight your way out of it." Gene Turney should know. He's done it day after day.

2. BOLD CONSERVATIVE

Leopold D. Silberstein of Penn-Texas

LEOPOLD D. SILBERSTEIN, PRESIDENT AND CHAIRMAN OF THE Board of Penn-Texas Corporation, is a true conservative in the operation of his huge corporation. In fact, his business record clearly shows that he has been a consistent and constructive builder of every enterprise with which he has been associated.

However, Silberstein flatly refuses to accept the type of conservatism which insists that the status quo must be maintained at all costs. He sees no reason why conservatism should fail to go hand in hand with bold leadership. He has observed too many companies lose their dominance to vigorous competition because their managements were blind to the dangers of everlastingly standing pat.

Another trait, and one that goes hand in hand with his bold conservatism, is Silberstein's ability and willingness to think and act independently of the crowd. This independent thinking he has successfully applied to many situations. Today's result is a successful industrialist in his fifties, a comparative newcomer to America, who already employs 12,000 people.

"I am not dealing with companies, I am dealing with people," says the man whose corporation owns or controls companies operating from coast to coast. Recent dramatic proof of his preoccupation with people was his offer of a thousand jobs to Hungarian refugees.

Leopold Silberstein was born in Berlin in 1904, the son of a well-to-do middle-class family. His father was an export banker who did well until World War I. Following the Armi-

13

stice, Germany was saddled with a staggering war debt. Inflation spiraled. Prices soared. Butter cost roughly the equivalent of eighteen dollars a pound, shoes several hundred dollars a pair. The family export banking business declined rapidly.

His keen mind eager for knowledge, young Silberstein went to work as a stock exchange runner at the age of sixteen. He learned on the job and used his income to complete his education in evening courses at the University of Berlin. Coming from a family in the banking business, it was natural that he should study economics. However, more than early environment led him to that field. "People have savings, and then suddenly they are wiped out. You become interested and want to get to the roots of it." Silberstein, a brilliant student, got to the roots of it through his studies and research—research that he continued when he left the exchange and went to work for a stockbroker.

At the age of eighteen, Silberstein was one of the youngest men to hold a seat on the Berlin Stock Exchange. Special permission was necessary for anyone under twenty-one to hold an exchange seat. His employer had to assume responsibility for his actions. Both conditions were met.

Inflation was now firmly in the saddle. Trading was in billions of marks. A "high-figure psychology" gripped Germany along with soaring prices. Paupers spoke in thousands; the man in the street in millions. A person would exchange his money for a cigarette lighter, not because he needed the lighter, but because it had a more real, unchanging value than his money!

It was a world as weird as Alice's Wonderland. Values in Germany were as topsy-turvy as anything Alice encountered. Conditions were not just expanding. They were exploding. Prices rose daily. A hundred thousand, a million, a billion marks —the value printed on the face of the paper meant little.

In the midst of such conditions there seemed no sound basis of value on which to build a future. Few people seemed able to cope with this topsy-turvy condition. Leopold Silberstein, already an independent thinker at the age of eighteen, was one of the few. His intensive study of foreign securities and foreign exchange had taught him comparative values—a form of knowledge unknown to many older heads.

Remembering those days, President Silberstein says, "Germany is an importing country. Germany has to import its food, its raw materials, everything. [He pronounces it "everysing!" with the emphasis of knowledge and conviction.] When you have to buy your raw material in foreign currency, especially when you are trying to recover from a war, you realize how poor you are. Here in the United States it is a different situation, you know. Germany lacked the needed production for recovery.

"Currency is only confidence," Silberstein continues, using one of the words that recur when he speaks about his business, "confidence and production. It isn't gold. In the face of these pressures, Germany had very little production and the people had almost no confidence. The currency simply had to go down."

Before he reached his nineteenth birthday, Leopold Silberstein had evolved a guiding principle that has stuck with him all his life. "You have to have real values. Money without production and confidence is just paper. Billions of marks—just paper. Dealing at this time on foreign markets, I came to believe in foreign securities. I didn't count any more in marks. I counted only in foreign—what you call hard currencies, hard money."

It is almost impossible to recapture the spirit of independent thinking that young Silberstein displayed. He flew in the face of the hysteria, the epidemic of high-figure psychology that gripped Germany. He had the incredible imagination to detach himself from the hectic local conditions. Instead, he dealt in small lots of foreign securities and foreign exchange. At the end of a week, when others counted their profits in millions, he counted his in ones, twos, tens. But the others counted in marks while Silberstein counted in francs, guilders, pounds, dollars. "There was my solid value," he recalls.

Despite the spongy softness of Germany's currency, the young man who searched for "real values" had great confidence in the ultimate future of Germany's economy. Silberstein believed implicitly in a return to normalcy. He felt, with an intensity that amounted to sure knowledge, that there would be a monetary reform. It would be accomplished, he reasoned, with a return to old and intrinsically sound values. In view of what lay ahead for the German economy, this was clear reasoning indeed, particularly for a youth of twenty. His sound thinking was destined to be vindicated. Silberstein decided to look around for one of his "real values."

"What did you do, Mr. Silberstein?"

"Safety first! I looked around—manufacturing, mining—this, that, and the other thing. It was difficult under inflationary conditions to determine the real value of a company. Under inflation, if the manager of a company sold out his stock of merchandise at the wrong time, he could bankrupt the company."

The then-current uncertainty of company values led the future philanthropist to the first commercial application of his ability to think independently of the crowd. He found that *a piece of property could be purchased for the same price as ten pairs of shoes!* Battalions of investors were aware of this astonishing fact, but they lacked one important ingredient in Silberstein's make-up: confidence in the return of solid values.

Armed with this confidence, Silberstein sought the advice of the best real-estate men in Berlin. He located good properties. Above all, he had the courage to buy them.

"If you don't have confidence in the future of your country, you should get out," is a remark he put into practice years later when war clouds mixed with persecution and conquest to turn Germany into an outlaw nation. Even in this early venture, Silberstein followed the formula that he applies today.

hundreds of older and presumably wiser heads reviewing every ramification of the investment market.

Germany's efforts to escape the inflationary spiral were successful. The mark regained its position among the monies of the world. No longer did street-corner vendors in New York sell "fresh" 10,000,000-mark bills for twenty-five cents. They became curios, demonetized playthings. The Alice that was Germany came out of the topsy-turvy Wonderland of soaring inflation. Prices were stabilized. Life settled down to normal.

Having startled the financial community twice during the previous hectic years, Silberstein did it again as Germany reached a plateau of normalcy in 1926. This time, however, he won the plaudits reserved for a grand master. He emerged in the new dawn of normalcy a wealthy real-estate owner.

The man whose pattern for success has worked as well in his adopted country as in the land of his birth gives much of the credit to the "experts." "I have used experts all my life," he says. "I cannot say that everything I have done on their advice has been 100 per cent right, but this I can say—nothing I have ever done has been a 100 per cent lemon!"

Still in his early twenties, Silberstein settled down to a conservative building of his real-estate empire. He married. Two children—Charles and Elizabeth—were born. The father could build a home for his children such as he remembered from his own comfortable, protected childhood. But the brilliant, active mind kept probing the business world for new fields to conquer, and another bright horizon came into view.

German textiles were "soft"—mills could be had relatively inexpensively. The country was reclaiming its export market, but fabrics found virtually no overseas buyers. Looms gathered dust as a new, curious, and inventive generation of German scientists turned their attention to machines and chemicals. But out of chemical research and experimentation a new fabric —rayon—was being born in the laboratories of one of Germany's giant corporations.

With confidence in the country's chemists and scientists, L. D. again thought independently, again bought in a "dead" market. Many a person *could* have done it; Silberstein *did* it. He bought a nearly valueless textile mill. When rayon was presented to an amazed world, the idle mill was rapidly converted to its production. Experienced textile workers were lured back from other jobs by their affection for their original occupation; unemployed mill hands jumped at the opportunity. Badly needed employment was provided. The business—a new, exciting outgrowth of one of the world's oldest crafts—was bound to boom. The venture was a complete success.

In the normalcy of the late twenties, he turned his spare-time attention to art, becoming a connoisseur. "In addition to the enjoyment I got out of owning them, I found that paintings were a better investment than anything on the stock exchange," says the art collector.

In 1934, L. D. made his first visit to the United States, which was later to become his adopted country. It was part of a long tour, made in the days before business associations and governmental agencies exchanged observation groups. He traversed both Europe and the Americas to compare production methods in other parts of the world with those in Germany. What he saw in America made his eyes pop as wide as he had ever popped the eyes of Germany's financiers.

Here was a country with ports, ships, natural resources, methods of distribution not dreamed of in Europe—and production techniques far ahead of the rest of the world. Yet, despite the wealth of natural blessings and man-made advances, this was a nation wallowing in a depression, hopeless, without confidence.

"I believed in America more than the people who were living here or were born here," Mr. Silberstein recalls. "To show my confidence, I bought some stock—oil and railroads. Not much, perhaps—but I bought stocks for half a dollar or

a dollar in 1938 that are now selling at a hundred or more."
Again, the key was confidence.

The visiting businessman spoke of threatening war in Europe. Hitler's star was rising. He had not yet dared to raise the gas chambers, but the specter of persecution had become a reality. "War will come," Silberstein told his newly made American friends.

"Hitler does not want a war," he was assured. "You see this from a persecution point of view. It simply means that big business is coming to power." Hitler was still a semicomic character, viewed from across the Atlantic. Only a handful of American prophets cried of war in a wilderness of public indifference. They were considered rather crotchety people and were disregarded.

With business dealings his "avocation" as well as his career, L. D. might have stayed in Germany a little longer. But having his children mocked and despised—no! Necessarily leaving behind him the great bulk of his wealth and possessions, Leopold Silberstein took his family to friendly Holland. Despite his belief that Hitler would set out on a chain of conquest, he remained optimistic. "The German people, I thought, would come to their senses. Another year or two, I told myself, and Hitler would be just another bad dream and we could go back."

That was the greatest error in judgment L. D. ever made. The "invincible" Wehrmacht spread over Europe. In gratitude to his temporary home country, Mr. Silberstein had joined the Dutch National Guard. For four pathetic days, the time it took the Nazi Wehrmacht to crush the tiny nation, the expatriate fought the war of Holland. The man who had taken his family to Holland as a stopping-off place on his way to the United States—he had hoped to emigrate to these shores when he left Berlin—refused to let his Dutch friends think that he would accept the hospitality of their country during the good days, then desert it during the bad.

"As soon as the war was lost, my commanding officer turned to me and said, 'Look here, if they get you, neither you nor your family will live very long.' There was nothing more I could do; I left.

"I got hold of my family and what money I could. That money I gave to the captain of a fishing boat to take us to England. On the way to the boat, I rounded up forty-one other Jews, and when the captain said he would sail to England, we all got aboard. Later I learned that the Gestapo got to my apartment in Amsterdam just about thirty minutes after we left.

"The trip to England usually takes a few hours. That trip took three days, and I found myself the commander of a ship. I had to ration the food. Who knew? The trip might have taken ten days. After the war I saw the captain of that boat. He was very grateful to me for getting him out of Holland."

German born, the Silbersteins were interned by the British; interned but safe. Subsequently, in line with policy, L. D. was shipped to an "enemy civilian" center in Australia.

"It was a very nice time. I was interned there for probably ten months behind barbed wire," says the man who had exchanged a real-estate empire for a chance to live. "I read, and kept in contact with the world, and every day I worked on my application to get out. Friends in England helped.

"Many things in life happen by chance, and you really have to be lucky," Silberstein states, as though luck were a talisman to all his previous years of planning and bold maneuvering. "The man who was sent to Australia by the British War Office to look over the cases he would release or ask to join the British Pioneers was a former stockbroker with a firm I did business with before the war. I was probably the first man he interviewed. I wrote, telling him who I was, and he got my release for me.

"I had to go to a neutral country when I was freed, so I went to China—Shanghai. There I did a little banking business, and the profits I sent to the refugee committees that were doing such wonderful work."

How does a newly released refugee, shipped to a faraway country, get into the banking business? "When I made my trip in 1934, I knew war was coming. 'What if I need money?' I asked myself, and the answer was to open some bank accounts. I bought South American bonds, in case I should land there. My main account I opened in America, where I arranged for a 'possible trust.'

"I said to the bank, 'If something ever happens that I cannot provide for my family, you use this to help them.' So my children were educated in England; the bank was very fine to do that, I think. My other accounts were in England and Portugal. Why Portugal? you may ask. The reason was the Pyrenees Mountains. The war, I figured, would never cross them. I was right. I was lucky. From the Portugal bank I arranged to get my funds in United States dollars. It was just a few thousand, but in China there was bad inflation and those dollars had a lot of value. So I became a banker in a small way.

"Before the dollars arrived, I lived in a hotel on credit. 'Give me checks to be cashed later,' the manager said. Later I cashed the checks myself. He was a nice fellow.

"Then the Japs came. They wanted to be business partners, so I went out of business. How could I work with the enemy? I decided to become a farmer."

Life on a farm appeared to the Shanghai former banker, as it does to many city-bred persons, a relaxed, assured way to live. The farm grew feed for the cows, chickens, and pigs. It would be a self-sustaining enterprise. There would be plenty of sleep, a good, comfortable living, even if it were at opposite poles to his past career.

"At three o'clock one morning I was awakened. All the chickens and pigs were sick. I found out that in farming, as in any other kind of business, you have to be prepared for the unexpected."

The bucolic dream was shattered, but Silberstein sustained himself until a six-month trip by way of the Suez Canal returned him to his family in England.

In 1948, the family hegira that had begun in 1938 finally came to an end; the Silberstein family came to the United States to make it their home. But the conclusion of one phase was the commencement of another. The confidence Silberstein had expressed in America in 1934 was increased when he reached these shores as an immigrant rather than simply as a visitor.

Within six years he was one of the country's best-known figures in business and investment circles. His name became known through a mountain of newspaper items, investment columns, editorials, business and news magazines, as well as a deep, wide ring of personal associations in such diverse fields as industry, art, yachting, and philanthropy.

Leopold Silberstein can outline his formula for success and give examples. He can set forth, with specific applications, the guiding rules of his climb up the ladder. But he fails to mention just one outstanding quality that helps set him apart as an eminent success in our competitive world: *the faculty to concentrate solely on the matter at hand.*

"L. D. called us to his home at six o'clock one Sunday morning for an emergency meeting," recalls one of his long-time American business asociates. "We stuck with that problem all day long. The five of us he had called in went home late in the evening. Well, you know how most of us are when we've been wrestling with an emergency all day—we go on turning it over in our minds most of the night.

"Monday morning we got to Mr. Silberstein's office, and we all looked as though the cat had dragged us in. Silberstein should have looked the same way. After all, he heads the company we were all worrying about ... but you know, he was the only one who was wide awake and well rested."

L. D. at this point picked up the conversation with "Well, when the men left, I said to myself, 'I certainly can't do anything more about the emergency tonight. Besides, I'll need a clear head tomorrow.' So I went to sleep."

The guiding rule that comes out of that story—although Mr. Silberstein never sums it up in just so many words—is concentration on the matter at hand, even if it is such a garden-variety matter as getting a good night's sleep.

Leopold D. Silberstein's annual report for 1956 lists the following nineteen companies and divisions: THE HALLICRAFTERS COMPANY (Electronics and Communications Equipment); PRATT AND WHITNEY COMPANY (Basic Machine Tools, Cutting Tools, Gages); "QUICK-WAY" TRUCK SHOVEL COMPANY (Truck-mounted Power Shovels); THE CRESCENT COMPANY (Automotive Wiring and Cable); CHANDLER EVANS (Aircraft Components); CAROL CABLE COMPANY DIVISION (Insulated Wire and Cable for Electrical and Industrial Markets); POTTER AND JOHNSTON COMPANY (Automatic Turret Lathes, Gilda Filling and Seaming Machines, Newark Gear Cutters); INDUSTRIAL BROWNHOIST CORPORATION (Heavy Materials-handling Equipment); ELYRIA FOUNDRY (Castings for the Machine Tool Trade); LIBERTY AIRCRAFT PRODUCTS CORPORATION (Aircraft Parts Manufacturers); COLT'S PATENT FIRE ARMS MANUFACTURING COMPANY (Manufacturers of Firearms); COLT'S PLASTICS COMPANY (Plastic Packaging Products and Custom Moldings); LOWELL INSULATED WIRE CORPORATION (Telephone, Communication Wire and Appliance Cord Sets); BAYWAY TERMINAL DIVISION (Terminal Operators); PENNSYLVANIA COAL AND COKE (Bituminous Coal Mining); CENTRAL ENGINEERING DIVISION (Aeronautical, Mechanical, and Electromechanical Engineering); SEABORNE AND SEASPLENDOR STEAMSHIP CORPORATIONS (Owners and Operators of Inter-continental Merchant Ships); PROPULSION TEST EQUIPMENT DIVISION (Design and Development of Test Equipment); NUCLEAR ENGINEERING DIVISION.

It's quite a list.

But the idea of Penn-Texas had not been born when the

new arrival started to work. At this point he says, "My greatest
assets were not my companies, they were my friends—all
around the world. I did not start here as a stranger."

He turned to his American friends, asking for the name of
the smartest real-estate man in New York City. Silberstein
went to him, asked his advice. It was given; it was *taken*. If a
man knows more than L. D. in a given field, he is listened to
with respect, and his suggestions become guides for action. So
L. D. listened, heeded, and prospered.

Germany, sane once more after Hitler's blood bath and reign
of horror, had returned L. D.'s real estate. Far from arriving
in the New World as a penniless refugee, he was again a substantial businessman, horrified by the things that had happened
in Europe and ready to carve a new productive career for himself in the United States, for which he had conceived a love
during his first visit here.

He listened, heeded, and prospered, but the old drive was
undimmed. The war was over, the suffering past, and the
energy he had displayed in the business world since the age of
sixteen reasserted itself. He grew restless in the easy role of
real-estate operator and rent collector. L. D. looked about for
new fields to conquer.

A survey of America's natural resources indicated to the
ambitious real-estate man that the country must eventually
fall back on its coal supply. The oil, according to the survey,
would go long before the coal. Germany had made oil from
coal; it would have to come back in value.

Once more the erstwhile Berlin businessman flew in the face
of general acceptance. Coal, by and large, is considered a "hot
potato," and an unprofitable one. Nevertheless, it held two
attractions for the newly interested investor, the independent
thinker.

First, coal was *basic*. Uninterested in the most promising
gadgets, which could become obsolete, Silberstein's belief in
true values led to a deep interest in basic industries. Second,

because it is a "hot potato," there is little if any competition in obtaining control of a coal company. Mr. Silberstein, nearly alone among industry leaders, gives credit to John L. Lewis for saving the coal industry. "He forced the mines to start mechanizing," he says. Despite Lewis and American ingenuity in mechanical fields, coal-mine mechanization had made little progress when L. D. decided, in 1951, that he would seek control of Pennsylvania Coal and Coke.

"People said, 'There must be a crazy man.' Nobody wanted a coal company. There was no fight. I got control."

Now it seems as though another person is talking. The businessman who had just gained control of a coal company in a swift coup changes as he says, "Now came my basic trouble. I was always afraid that something would happen to the miners. I took the mines out of the red, but made sure that we didn't save one cent on our safety program. We took the water out of the mines. We put in sprinklers and dust collectors. We got the safety award in Central Pennsylvania for not losing one man. We didn't lose money, but we made only a few thousand profit that year. But, most important, we didn't lose one man. There was never a wildcat strike, and we won the safety award. The miner is interested in one thing—when he goes down, that he also comes back. They must have known we looked for safety first.

"We never had to be told to comply with safety regulations when the mines were inspected—we had better regulations than those required by law. Some of the regulations they actually copied from us."

Pennsylvania Coal and Coke is more than a story of safety. It is more than the turning of a notorious money-losing industry into a profit maker. Going once again to the experts, this time in the field of mine mechanization, Silberstein had them construct "continuous miners" adapted to the needs of his company. This is a complex machine roughly as far advanced beyond the electric saw as the electric light is beyond the candle.

The enlightened mine-area youth of the forties was away from the fields where the men of their families had swung a pick for generations. Compulsory education and a changing age promised to turn the mining area into ghost towns. With two brilliant strokes, the exodus was stemmed. First, there was an award-winning safety program. Second, L. D. opened a "mining mechanics" school to teach youths how to run the modern continuous miner that released their hands from the pick.

Apparently the plan was working to the satisfaction of everyone from miner to stockholder. Then came a blow. "Oil and natural gas—they began to pipe them all over the country at that time, you know. They were beating us down. I still had confidence in coal, but 'if you cannot beat them, join them,' so we went into the oil-producing business.

"It was our first idea of diversification. In industry, I believe we were the first publicly to use the word 'diversification.' We spread out, but remained in basic industry. That way you make better use of your engineering talent. But before we went into oil, we did one other thing."

The "one other thing" is a re-enactment of the early Silberstein. With the domestic coal market evaporating on the one hand and his mechanized mines capable of high production on the other, he saw Europe as his best remaining market. That required ships. L. D. had none. Now comes the re-enactment:

The coal-company president selected the two ships he wanted. Armed only with their sales price in his mind, he called on companies likely to be on the market to charter cargo ships. He arranged for "bare boat" charters with two such firms. Each charter was for five years; payments were to be made monthly. "I suddenly found out that you could get back twice your money—two times the cost of the ships—in five years," Silberstein relates, still with a note of surprise in his voice. Now, armed with the charters, he visited banks. From one of them, using the charters as security, he obtained the down-payment money required to buy the ships. "We taught the banks to lend money against a charter contract."

Another ship was added to the small fleet. Later one was sold at a profit. "We now have two ships that cost us nothing, earn terrific income, and have a value between two and two and a half million dollars."

One condition of the charter contract, of course, was that Pennsylvania Coal and Coke's products ride in the hulls to the European markets.

"The next step was oil," L. D. recounts. "It's the same story. Some very interesting properties were offered to us in Texas. What did I know about oil? I looked for the expert, and everybody told me that man was Bill Moody. He can just smell oil as he goes along. We bought the properties together. He became president."

The laconic "We bought the properties together" covers the events more in the style of a raincoat than in that of a sweater. It does the job, but neglects the interesting details.

L. D. approached Moody concerning the "interesting properties" but not before he had been to the oil expert of a New York bank—naturally a Texan himself—and suggested that he would go into partnership with Moody, and that they might want some financing. "By chance," says L. D., "Moody had an account at that bank, so naturally they wanted to favor him.

"Nobody was worried about company management. Bill Moody, like his father, is almost a legend to oilmen. The bank promised the financing."

The bank that had advised Silberstein financed the company. The bank received fifty shares of stock; the balance was to be paid in oil payments. From three and a half million dollars a few years ago, the debt is well below a million, and the oil company has grown from one hundred to a hundred and sixty oil and gas properties.

In his search for experts, L. D. had invited Oscar Chapman —President Truman's Secretary of the Interior—to join the board of Penn-Texas as a consulting director. Chapman, he felt, was the authoritative expert on natural resources. As events developed, the former cabinet member served as far more than that.

Both Board Chairman Silberstein and Consulting Director Chapman were among the guests invited to a luncheon in 1953 for the benefit of Korean orphans. Another distinguished guest was to be Robert Young, who was preparing at that time to battle for control of the New York Central Railroad. Chapman knew Young. Silberstein knew he would meet the dynamic railroad man; and from that meeting he planned to build and diversify Penn-Texas' holdings beyond its coal-oil-gas-ships range.

Luncheon and formalities over, Silberstein casually asked Young if he would like to sell his Industrial Brownhoist stock. Industrial Brownhoist is a long-established, successful Ohio and Michigan corporation. Mr. Young owned 48 per cent of its stock. It was logical to assume that he might be willing to sell that stock in view of his pending New York Central battle.

"Do you want to buy it?" Young inquired.

"Yes," said Silberstein. "How much do you want?"

"Thirteen dollars a share," was the answer.

"On what terms?"

"Let's work them out tomorrow."

They shook hands and parted. The following day terms were arranged—$500,000 in cash, the balance of $2,500,000 in three-year notes. Silberstein then went into the market, bought another 3 per cent of Industrial Brownhoist stock, and had control of the company.

This luncheon transaction was not nearly so casual as it appears. There was a great deal of advance preparation. Knowing that he was to meet the industrialist who was about to be engaged in a titanic proxy fight, Silberstein investigated his holdings. From a Penn-Texas director who had once been engaged in a proxy battle with Young, he learned how the man would be likely to act. In addition, he learned that Industrial Brownhoist had a cash reserve of thirteen dollars for every share of its stock, "so everything in the company I just got for nothing!"

The balance of the purchase price, incidentally, was paid off in eighteen months, just half the allotted time.

"Young was quick," Silberstein recalls, "and I was prepared to be just as quick as he was. This transaction gave us $6,000,000 in assets, mostly in cash, and helped us to buy Niles-Bement-Pond Company, which is now the Pratt and Whitney Machine Tool Company."

There was a battle in West Hartford before Silberstein gained control of that company. Rumors flared up that the plant would be moved to Kentucky. Workers and the press became panicky. Time proved the complete falsity of the rumors. Pratt and Whitney expanded. It is the plant that is absorbing the bulk of the Hungarian refugees who are employed by Penn-Texas.

Himself a refugee hounded halfway around the world not many years before, Silberstein radiated a glow of happiness at being able to provide jobs for the skilled, schooling for the unskilled, and help in every way until they "got on their feet."

With the acquisition of Niles-Bement-Pond, it could be said that Silberstein's industrial empire had really "arrived." Certainly by early 1954 Silberstein's Pennsylvania Coal and Coke Corporation had become a broadly diversified industrial operation. Its original name was no longer descriptive. Consequently, at the annual stockholders' meeting held on April 29 of that year, it was voted to change the name to Penn-Texas Corporation.

Incidentally, warm regard for Silberstein had grown in Hartford long before the refugee-job program showed his heart. When Connecticut was struck by raging floods in the midsummer of 1955, Silberstein was the first industrialist to offer concrete relief to the victims. His gift of $25,000 through Niles-Bement-Pond was the bellweather of a cascade of gifts. But he was first. Another reason is well expressed in the Award of Achievement presented to L. D. by the Washington, D.C., Advertising Club on March 19, 1956. The award commended his "outstanding corporate information program, based on the belief that the investing, working, and consuming publics alike 'have the right to know' how America's leading corporations operate."

From his earliest days, as evinced by his first Berlin real-estate transactions, Silberstein has never been interested in what he describes angrily as the "fast buck." His philosophy leads him to build, consolidate, improve. "I often have willingly waited to see the fruits of my ideas," he says. He has no patience with the type of man (happily rare) who moves in on a company, reorganizes from top to bottom, fires skilled personnel, curtails research and maintenance to show an increase in profits, then sells a sick company for an inflated profit. His is the philosophy of retaining good administrators, key personnel, and "top brass" along with the working force. He makes changes only when they will help the firm, increase sales, increase production, and improve conditions for everyone, from stockholder to shipping clerk.

There are new athletic facilities for the workmen at the West Hartford factory, together with a new field house. The Hungarians who elected to come to Hartford (many others were absorbed by Penn-Texas plants throughout the country) were to become acquainted with other Europeans—forty young men brought to America to learn our way of getting things done so that American "know-how" might become an asset in countries needing it.

Well-prepared food is served with deference in good restaurants today to the man who remembers his first chocolate bar at the age of sixteen. If he dines in a particular midtown New

York restaurant, Silberstein reminds the headwaiter to fix a bag of *petits fours* for him to take to the girls in his office. A business transaction of great importance may be the purpose of the luncheon meeting, but the boss remembers the sweets for the staff.

Adding up so detailed a career in a few thousand words must necessarily leave much unsaid. The over-all pattern appears to be immensely complex: A boy prodigy, self-made, wiped out, and fortune recouped before his twenty-first birthday. Hounded halfway around the world, his businesses uprooted by warmakers. A refugee, an escapee, a D. P., an immigrant. But, above all, a bold, independent thinker.

Leopold Silberstein, in the course of conversation, sets forth a number of rules he has lived by—keys to success on the key chain of his career. Here they are:

First, have *confidence*—in your country and its economy as well as in yourself. Second, concentrate on *basic industries*—steel, copper, coal. (Incidentally, Silberstein's confidence in coal was seconded on a coast-to-coast television program by Cyrus Eaton, who is generally referred to as "the last tycoon.") Third, go in for the *long pull*, not the "fast buck." ("Business is like fishing," says L.D. "You have to have patience.")

Fourth, *understand business*. Study it and your studies will be rewarded. Fifth, *specialize*. ("If I make a machine anyone can make, my competition hounds me, but if I am highly specialized, then I have no competition.")

Silberstein's next four keys are *determination, courage, judgment,* and *careful planning*. These elements are well integrated in his own character and career.

"You must know your materials. Study them. Know everything about them—what they can do, their history, what they can do in the future," says L.D. "And you must have the ability to make the right decisions."

A handful of rules and the ability to think apart from the crowd. These enabled him to succeed in his first real-estate venture, to obtain the ships he needed, to enter the oil and gas business. One thing more: the everlasting alert ability to concentrate on the matter at hand—whether it is remembering cookies for his secretary, getting his needed sleep, or applying himself to adding a new company to the growing empire of his Penn-Texas Corporation.

3. SHE FOUND OUT FOR HERSELF

Mrs. B. A. Coleman of B. F. Gladding

A BEAUTIFULLY GOWNED WOMAN WAS IN ATLANTA'S NUMBER-one sporting-goods store, talking earnestly to one of the clerks. Her Hattie Carnegie attire, topped by a John Frederics hat, appeared out of place among the fishing rods and guns. Looking more at home in the masculine atmosphere, a ruddy-faced man in an open-neck shirt stepped up to the counter and interrupted the woman.

"I want a fishing line," he said to the clerk.

"Yes, sir. What kind?"

"Oh, any kind. Going to do a little fly casting."

The woman turned with slow dignity toward the customer. "Any kind!" she exclaimed. "I think you want a *Gladding* line." With that introduction, she launched into a brief but well-documented talk describing the lines, the types he should have for different types of sports fishing, the reasons why Gladding lines surpassed all others.

The Atlanta incident is not common in the life of Mrs. Coleman. She is vice-president in charge of sales and advertising of B. F. Gladding and Company, America's oldest manufacturer of fishing lines for sports fishermen. But if the incident is not common, it is at least typical of the way Billie Coleman charges in to meet any problem—whether it be in the sales, production, or policy making of the Gladding organization.

Perhaps the company should be called an institution rather

than an organization. It is the sole commercial enterprise of
South Otselic, located in the beautiful Otselic Valley of western
New York, forty miles from Syracuse. Appropriately enough,
the state's largest bass hatchery is the town's other claim to
fame. "Other" is the wrong word. South Otselic has one more
claim to fame: that is the way in which Billie Coleman, probably the most energetic grandmother of the century, has come
to typify a business concern and an entire community to the
rest of the country.

Sporting-goods buyers, business executives, sports and feature
writers, and sporting fishermen and women from Canada to
Bimini, from Maine to California, know the attractive, dynamic
Billie. To wholesale dealers in every state she *is* the B. F. Gladding Company.

In a traditionally masculine segment of a world that is com-
monly referred to as "a man's," the reasons and ways behind
Mrs. Coleman's achievement are an encouraging revelation—
a revelation of the way in which interest and spirit can combine to produce success.

At the death of Mrs. Coleman's first husband, Keith Angell,
who was president of the Gladding Company, the then Mrs.
Angell was left a widow to raise a ten-year-old son—and to all
outward appearances, this would present no difficulties. She
had inherited nearly a third of Gladding Company's stock, and
the company had paid a dividend every year for a century
and a quarter. She owned a comfortable home. Economically,
the picture looked rosy.

South Otselic is a small town. It has about three hundred
fifty inhabitants. Nearly half of them—the major working force
of the town and its environs—work for Gladding. Gladding
employees form the volunteer fire department (and get paid
when they leave their machines to put out a blaze). They form
most of "the biggest little" chamber of commerce in the country. In a word, everybody knows everybody else. So there is
no wonder in the fact that Mrs. Coleman was kept up to date,

day to day, on everything that happened in the fishing-line plant, even though her visits to it were few and far between.

From reports, she heard that all was not well with the firm. Cost consciousness was overruling common sense. On a personal basis, this translated itself into jeopardy for herself, her son, her friends—the many neighbors who worked for Gladding. It took nothing more than her woman's intuition to tell her that the company could be closed up by a cost-accounting system that saw no further than the red and black figures in a ledger.

But Mrs. Coleman also knew that a small town hatched rumors galore, most of them strangers to the truth. The Gladding Company, of course, was the focal point of nearly all tall tales in South Otselic, and Billie decided the only way to find out what was what was to go to see for herself. So she went, and she stayed.

Billie's business knowledge and ambitions were apparently nil. She had been a piano prodigy at Rochester's Eastman School of Music, but had relinquished a possible career in music to become a homemaker. She had attended conferences and exhibits with her late husband, and had "eaten, slept, and drunk" fishing lines. But as to her knowledge of exactly how they were made, promoted, priced—the multiple details of manufacturing and distribution—"I didn't know *that* about it," she says with a snap of her fingers.

It seems a rather incongruous background on which to base a successful business career. As the wife of a company president, many a woman could attend exhibits and conferences until her last days without learning anything of practical use about the business her husband was in, or the industry as a whole. Billie, thanks to her interest in things and people, was a length or two ahead in that respect. Nevertheless, the wife of a company president rarely gets in on the ground floor of production, packing, inspection, discussions of minute changes in machine operation, and location.

Billie demanded a place on the ground floor, a job in the factory. "After all," she explains, "I thought I certainly ought to know something about a company I owned a third of!"

"You'll be a troublemaker," she was told in just so many words. That opinion, she realized, was right. She wanted to make trouble—trouble for the segment of management that would consider cost accounting above quality, that would place today's profit above tomorrow's reputation. However, the widow of the company president realized that she could do little with her ideas until she had a more thorough understanding of what made the business tick.

The woman who had a long-range plan for rehabilitating the fishing-line company started on the most common job of them all. She went to work, punching the clock faithfully by seven every morning for more than a year, as a braid tender. There are more than two thousand braiding machines in the plant, turning out more than one hundred and fifty million yards of fishing line a year. Each of these carries eight, twelve, or sixteen spools of natural or synthetic fiber. The spools dance an intricate step around a central core of thread, like children running around a Maypole. The din of a thousand machines fills the braiding room where Billie went to work. It was hard on the ears of a woman accustomed to comfort, especially an ex-pianist, but determination kept her at the braiders.

Among the very real considerations that sent the future Mrs. Coleman to work, there was an important intangible: tradition. To her fellow workers, because of her Gladding-Angell family connection, Billie represented the company that had provided employment to South Otselic since 1816. It was Gladding that had brought job security, electricity, fire-fighting equipment to South Otselic. Farmers still come to the Gladding machine shop with broken equipment and use its facilities without charge. When the War Between the States "softened" Union currency, old John Gladding bartered fishing lines for food— food for everybody in town. Woodrow Wilson gave the company special permission to use scarce materials during World War I for "national security"; during World War II, the government had not rejected a single parachute line braided in South Otselic. Grace Brown of Dreiser's *An American Tragedy* had worked in the braiding rooms. B. F. Gladding and Company and the town in which it is situated are as tightly interwoven as one of its own braided lines. Without the company, another American tragedy could be written about the town.

There was something incongruous about driving to an eighteen-dollar-a-week job in a Cadillac. Billie left the car at home and bicycled to work. By the time she graduated from the braiding room to the stock room, she knew how every kind of fishing line was made—and why.

In the stock room she found a conglomeration of new, old, and discontinued lines. "It was a mess. I set up the stock room we have now, and I put in the stock myself. When I went over to work in the office, I worked out the visible index system so we could control our production to match orders. Now everybody wonders how in the world we did it in the old days. But before I got over to the office, I worked in the inspection department.

"That was a mess, too. In running the plant strictly on a cost-accounting basis, they had put the inspectors on a piecework basis. Inspectors got paid for the amount of line they inspected, so of course they let little things go through that they would have rejected if they were being paid a regular salary. This seemed so obvious to me, I raised the devil about it. It was one of the first things I changed. I guess it made them think they were right when they said I'd be a troublemaker!"

About the time Mrs. Coleman moved into the office, illness forced top-management retirements that left two or three vital jobs wide open. One of these—vice-president in charge of sales and advertising—was given to the ex-braid tender. It was given her with the thought that it was better to have somebody—

anybody—in the position than have it vacant. Not the most
inspiring way to be handed a responsible job. But the "let's-
give-it-to-anybody" faction had not reckoned with Billie's will,
Billie's feeling toward the company and community, Billie's
vigor and personality, her indomitable "git up and go."

In short order she was known to sporting-goods buyers in
Atlanta, Chicago, Miami, New York, Boston, Los Angeles,
Portland. Name any wholesale sporting-goods center; she
visited it. To hear it in the lady's own words, there was nothing
to it. According to Billie Coleman, she hasn't done a thing. "It's
just that I'm the only woman who drops in to see these people,
and they're so surprised, they buy fishing lines."

"Then why is it," she was asked, "that other women can
succeed to big jobs, where women are scarce, and fail?"

"Don't know," is the only answer. The vice-president who
can talk by the hour about fishing lines cannot talk about herself. The buyer of fishing tackle for New York City's foremost
sporting-goods store sums up Billie Coleman's success in this
way: "There are several things that make Billie a good salesman. First of all, she's a lady. Oh, she can be 'one of the boys,'
but she's still a lady. She believes in her company and her
product so sincerely that everybody she talks to believes in
them, too. She knows what it's all about—knows fishing lines.
But maybe this is even more important: when she doesn't know
the answer to something you ask her, by God she says so!"

The obvious impact made on the buyer by Billie's occasional
admission of ignorance indicates that it is an asset anyone can
have in his personality account. Mrs. Coleman carries it a step
further. She gets the answer—and always has it for future reference. If the buyer in Atlanta repeats the question asked in
New York, she is there with the reply.

Billie has rolled up hundreds of thousands of air and rail
miles since succeeding to the vice-presidency of B. F. Gladding
and Company. She calls on customers, attends trade shows, and
fishes in tournaments from the Atlantic to the Pacific. Wher-

ever she travels, she carries her dynamic zeal, and even illness does not interfere—she won't permit it.

"There was that time in Chicago," she recalls, lingering over the name of the city as it brought back memories of the ordeal she encountered there several years ago. "I was sick as a pup. Couldn't get out of bed. Doctor wouldn't let me—you know what doctors are like.

"I'd made ever so many appointments. Here at nine o'clock. There at ten. Next place at a quarter to eleven, and so on through the afternoon, too.

"The doctor was going to shoot me if I got out of bed, and there were all those nice people expecting me. So I picked up the phone at nine in the morning and called the first person I had an appointment with. Said to him, 'Mr. Smith, this is Billie Coleman. I'm just as much in your office when I'm on this phone as if I were there in person.'

"Called them all and said the same thing. They were the nicest people. Took care of all my business and obeyed the doctor's orders, too—but the son of a gun didn't spoil my trip to Chicago!"

Incidents like this, multiplied year in and year out, add up to a graphic explanation of why Gladding line sales have literally quadrupled since Billie's been at her desk.

Back at home, you may find the lady engaged in any of a number of occupations or pastimes—but all of them related somehow to the Gladding Company or fishing. Take, for example, the unusual collection of fishing prints that adorn the walls of the Coleman home. Both Billie and her husband, Jim, find time whenever they are in a distant city to browse for additions to the collection that has spilled over to decorate walls in the Gladding office and factory. Rare Currier and Ives prints rub frames with French and English prints of a bygone day.

Hearing of Mrs. Coleman's dynamic energy and success, it would be natural to suppose that she is a person who has little time for "the other fellow"—a thought that points up still another side of her personality.

One day Billie was in conference with the other members of Gladding's top brass, her public-relations counsel, and three or four high-powered visitors. It was a highly important business meeting in every sense of the words. Her telephone rang.

"Yes?" she asked. "Certainly," she said, then turned to her associates and visitors and excused herself for a few minutes. Once out of her office, Billie ran to the factory to remind one of the girls not to forget to pick up a gallon of cider on her way home. The girl and her mother were giving a small party that night, and it just wouldn't be right if the cider were forgotten!

And Billie's concern for the comfort and security of the Gladding community reaches straight to its business heart. Through her efforts the employees today enjoy a mutual profit-sharing plan as well as medical insurance coverage.

Any day in the week the Coleman home may be converted into a social center-hotel for visitors to a town that has neither. Billie will arrive home a few minutes before the visitors are expected, brew coffee, mix drinks, and arrange the famous food she has somehow always managed to prepare "the day before" with an ever-ready assist from neighbors. With her amazing reserve of energy, it seems to take very little out of this dynamic woman to be gracious at home—every inch the hostess— after a full day's work. Guests enjoy themselves in her company, and Billie obviously enjoys them. It comes as a surprise to find that she is still the efficient businesswoman when without consulting her watch she turns to a guest and says, "If you want to catch that plane from Syracuse, you'd better check the time."

The guest checks his watch and finds it's time to go. Thinking it over on the drive back to Syracuse, his surprise diminishes. The sprightly lady of the fishing lines *always* displays the same efficiency, whether she is in her office or home, playing the role of executive or hostess, ensconced behind a high-piled desk or sparkling coffee table.

The home on the hill in South Otselic lives today in the promise that seemed so obvious years ago. Then, no one would have suspected the delicate economic thread on which it hung. Ease and plenty would have been taken for granted. The years have treated the home well. There is plenty. Ease? That depends on your definition of the word. The atmosphere can be called one of ease—but it wasn't easy. Interest and determination were held steadfast through hard years, long hours, and tough situations by Billie Coleman—"no bigger than a minute" —to fulfill the early dreams.

4. THE PUBLIC BE SERVED

Augustus B. Weller of Meadow Brook
National Bank

IF YOU WERE APPROACHED BY A BOARD OF DIRECTORS AND ASKED
to become the president of a bank, your reaction would probably be similar to that of Augustus B. ("Gus") Weller.

"I was intensely flattered," he recalls. "Being a bank president appealed to me as the acme of prestige, dignity, and public
approval."

What did he think about the work involved? "I expected to
go to the bank about ten each morning, enjoy a long lunch
each noon, with the pleasure of a friendly golf game two or
three afternoons each week. I expected to be an inspirational
public-relations front, building up new accounts on the golf
course through social contacts or old, established friendships."

The First National Bank of Merrick, situated in semi-rural
Nassau County on New York's Long Island, offered the presidency to Mr. Weller in May 1934. The previous president had
died the same month of a heart attack. There were five employees in the bank, none capable of assuming the mantle of
the presidency.

Despite the condition of Merrick's First National, typical of
thousands of banks in that depression year of '34, the original
attitude of the board of directors in selecting a new president
can be pointed to as outstanding. They wanted a man who was
known and respected in the community, a man who was a go-
getter, a man above reproach.

Gus Weller had moved to Merrick seven years before. Until

44

the crash, he had been with a bond house, first as a salesman, then in various executive capacities, including that of sales manager. Many a Yale graduate before him had sold bonds for a year or two, exhausted the purchasing power of his friends, and moved into other fields. Weller had not sold that way. He was thankful for the big sales, but found his real bread and butter in the small repeat purchaser. A lot of his business was transacted across the kitchen tables on Long Island farms.

Leaving the virtually dead field of bond selling, Weller formed his own advertising business. When the president of the First National Bank died of a heart attack, Weller was in the process of selling the business, retaining certain interests in its future development. Naturally the prospect of a "soft" job looked good, with its promise of prestige and golf. In 1934, who would turn down the opportunity of having his country-club membership paid for as a business expense?

Did the job meet expectations? Today the president of the bank, now the Meadow Brook National Bank, says, "If I had been more familiar with commercial banking operations, procedures, and public-relations attitudes, I surely would have run away from my friends who proposed the idea."

Gus Weller was in for several rude awakenings. First, he was to learn that a bank closes only its outer doors at three in the afternoon. Work goes on long after the last customer leaves.

Second, he had to learn bank operation. "I was naïve enough," he recalls, "to think it was simply standard operational procedure for a bank quickly and automatically to prove out its operations to the penny at the close of each working day." Instead, he learned that nothing was "automatic." Balancing the books became tedious reality. The lights burning in the bank at 3 A.M. had not been left on by mistake. And sometimes the bank's balance was achieved only by what Weller recalls as "certain adjustments which seemed to me that the difference was being carried over to the next day's work."

The man could adjust to those things. There were reasons for the tedious work, for the abbreviated lunch periods on busy days that contrasted sharply with his picture of long, sociable meals. But there was one matter to which he could not adjust, one thing about the First National he could not accept. That was the attitude of the staff—and of bankers in general—that "customers were to be treated only as necessary annoyances."

Weller's colleagues suffered from as many misconceptions about banking as he had. The prevailing attitude was that, since the customers did not understand banking procedures, they were to be told what to do in no uncertain terms. If they were able to summon up enough courage to ask questions, they were to be answered as curtly and as briefly as possible.

The man who had sold bonds over a mug of country coffee on a bare kitchen table had not used that attitude. The man who had built a successful advertising business had not built on that foundation. And even the dazzle of the title "bank president" could not blind him to the crying need that existed for better customer relations.

President Weller sat at a desk on the main banking floor, where he could see and be seen. What he saw one day became a turning point in the history of Merrick's First National Bank.

Several changes had already been made by the new president. He had persuaded three directors to resign. They had been replaced by young, interested, better-known businessmen. There were long discussions with each of the five employees, who made no secret of their discontent. Banking hours were from seven forty-five in the morning to three in the afternoon on weekdays, and until 1:00 P.M. on Saturdays. Those were the hours known to the public; there were numerous other working hours for the staff. It was years since anyone in the bank had had a raise in pay. Everyone on the staff knew that the bank was losing money, not promising a bright future.

One of Weller's first actions was to put through token increases. But even the new management with its greater interest in the individual, the prospect of a brighter future, and salary increases could not change the basic attitude of "the public be damned."

A customer had a difference of opinion with the bank's cashier. The difference of opinion became an argument. Their voices rose. President Weller looked up from the papers on his desk in time to see his cashier reach through the teller's window to grab the customer by the collar. In return, the customer was swinging both fists, as intent on performing mayhem as the cashier. It was time to do something besides act as a referee.

A patient's fever indicates that there is something wrong with him besides high body temperature. The fever heat of the fight in the bank indicated to Weller that there was more wrong with the establishment than a mere difference of opinion.

The Saturday closing hour was moved back to noon. Perhaps an added hour on the weekend and the indication that bank management was aware of the fact that the employees were *people* would help. Then another idea—new, novel, and nearly untried in those days—presented itself. Weller tells of it in these words:

"I discussed the problem with a friend of mine who was an officer in a large bank in New York City. He had learned banking in London. He said that he had also experienced arrogance and indifference on the part of the employees in his department in New York City. His conclusion was that the attitude was owing to the fact that the employees were greatly overworked in a monotonous routine and were not treated as individuals worthy of personal consideration.

"In a desperate attempt to break through the barrier of negative thinking, he had established the old English custom of four-o'clock tea in his department every afternoon. He thought it had helped a great deal and recommended it.

"I was willing to try anything. Remember, I was desperate, too. So we started having four-o'clock tea—twenty minutes of tea and cookies, with no discussion of business or customers permitted.

"At first the staff approached the idea with skepticism. They obviously thought it was sissified. But our group had increased to eight, and then nine, and the newcomers seemed to enjoy it from the first. Soon everyone looked forward to that break at 4 P.M.

"Through that tea break, or perhaps I should say because of it, the spirit of the organization changed. The people seemed to take pride in their work. They found a certain happiness in the camaraderie which reflected itself to our customers. We began to get back accounts which had left us for banks in neighboring communities because of discourtesies received at our bank.

"By the time World War II came along, we had an enthusiastic, aggressive, and well-coordinated group of fifteen, and we were able to extend some considerable help to the war effort."

When Weller assumed the presidency, the bank had $800,000 in deposits, $200,000 in capital, and a deficit of nearly $78,000. Today its assets are in excess of $296,000,000, with capital funds of $18,000,000 and reserve for losses of $3,700,000. Not bad for a man whose business-career parents had been bond sales and advertising. The bank has not only opened four additional offices, but extended its influence and Operation Success through thirteen mergers. The customer-minded president had to do more than serve tea and cookies to accomplish that!

How did he do it?

Banking is a strange world to most of us. When a bank is in the newspapers, the story is usually filled with astronomical figures. A quarterly statement of condition and an annual report are cold columns of unintelligible numbers that balance out to the penny. Each quarter the figures grow larger; that seems to be normal banking procedure. Yet many banks disappear. Few fail today, but aggressive banks with a plan for attracting customers grow through mergers. Gus Weller's bank is one of the growing kind. The key to its success, the answer

Weller consulted a piece of paper. "It brought our
｝ $23,718,386.30 and our capital to $1,824,371.87.
｡ a jump.

ﾷt was an incorporated village and a much larger
｜ than Merrick. Nevertheless, the merger was a
｣. The Freeport bank, with its charter dating back
ﾺd a considerable amount of uninvested funds that
ﾳed to meet the increasing demands for consumer-
ﾳcing.

ﾺmmunities of Freeport and Merrick are separated by
ﾺoundary, a brook that runs from the middle of the
ﾷn to the Atlantic Ocean. It's called the Meadow
ﾺl seemed to provide an appropriate name for the
ﾺanking institution, which would now operate offices
ﾺes of it."

ﾺh of the following year Meadow Brook completed
｜ merger, absorbing the West Hempstead National

ﾺhen," says President Weller, "our organization has
ﾺm the original five to 950, whom we believe to be
ﾺhusiastic, and aggressive employees. Many of them
ﾺin the numerous activities of a well-organized em-
ﾺub."

ﾺn who placed such emphasis on customer relations
ﾺd internal relations form the base for good public
ﾺWe believe that our welfare policies and our recog-
ﾺe dignity of each individual have formed one of the
ﾺeystones for our progress."

ﾺyou measure a bank's success?

ﾺcriterion is size, the Meadow Brook National Bank
ﾺeing counted among the first hundred of the coun-
ﾺo commercial banks. If the standard is money—
ﾺBrook holds the responsibility for nearly three hun-
ﾺon dollars, including the stock investment of 8,500
ﾺwomen, mostly residents of the area served by the

to "how did he do it?" is uncommonly simple for so complex a
business as commercial banking.

Weller set out to serve and please his customers.

Who were they? As any businessman must, a banker has to
know his typical customer if he is going to serve him as Gus
Weller planned to do.

Nassau County, along with a large part of Long Island, was
destined for one of the greatest real-estate and building booms
the country ever witnessed. But neither Gus Weller nor any
of his new directors knew that in the despondent mid-thirties.
What he did was build a bank that was able to grow to national
significance in the forties and fifties by dealing with the realities
of the thirties.

The bank's customers were small businessmen—men in retail
business for the most part, farmers—some of whom still drove
a horse to the bank in the thirties—and average middle-class persons. The latter made up the bulk of the bank's customers.

When the board of directors chose Gus Weller to be president, even they could not foresee how his bond-selling days
would influence his attitude toward "small" customers. In looking for his "average" customer, Weller recalls, "I remembered
the friendship and sincerity of the so-called little man and determined to cultivate him as a customer."

That determination became the First National's personal loan
department. Weller offered small loans based on character and
ability to repay rather than a financial statement.

Set down in just so many words, Weller's action loses a great
deal of its significance. It must be regarded against the then-
prevailing background, which included these elements:

First, the general "public-be-damned" attitude of banks and
bankers toward the "little man." Second, the fact that that attitude was being overcome but slowly in his own institution.
Third, despite the general attitude of banks toward personal
loans, Merrick is on the fringe of the country's most competitive money market. Fourth, a general air of discouragement

engendered by the great depression. Fifth, the fact that few of his potential customers could present a financial statement that would be accepted by most banks. Sixth, bankers who pioneer or introduce novelties must have the courage to face criticism by a legion of conservative bankers.

Against all that the man weighed his understanding and belief in people. And there was one bit of reasoning in his decision that *could* be understood by his more hardheaded peers. By spreading the bank's risk over many instead of among a few large borrowers, the matter of repayment became less subject to the fluctuations of one or another phase of the economy.

Had Weller made the right decision?

The question bothered him as the bank's investment money dwindled in small loans, but with faith in his decision he stuck to the small-loan program. Individual monthly payments poured in from a hundred borrowers, five hundred, several thousand. Earnings and income were up. And the customers gave the First National Bank an unexpected dividend. They opened checking accounts; they sent friends to the bank that believed in people. There is an old joke about banks with personal-loan departments—you can get a loan only when you can prove that you don't need it. Weller's attitude and action proved that the old wheeze did not apply to *his* bank.

Other bankers were quizzical and critical. "When are you going to hang three balls over the front door, Gus?" became a usual question for them to ask. Gus kept his temper, the bank kept its customers. And grew. Grew beyond the size anyone would expect of a bank in a suburban community of 5,000 souls.

The First National Bank of Merrick made its first F. H. A. Home Modernization loan toward the end of 1934. It was a ground breaker, the first such loan ever made in Nassau County. The following year the bank made its first personal loan. It should be recorded that these transactions launched a program —a program that expanded into the greatest single contributing

factor, fifteen years later,
ment of what is now the N

The small First National
that other banks would neit
of banking's conservative
most influential bank in N
known and felt from one
Deposits increased—slowly
War II—from $800,000 to

"Following the war," V
fast. We found our count
rapidly increasing populati
dustrial and commercial ac

"We realized our bank
in deposits, to meet the c
large loans and for other ba
on the part of Weller an
earned enough to retire the
and to pay a dividend to cc
an issue of new shares, plac
healthy condition.

"By 1948 we realized tha
have to expand through c
wanted to remain independ
New York City banking ins
covetous eyes on Nassau C
into the state legislature tha
lished banking district lines
to branch out into our cou

"Unless we grew and de
asset position, we would r
banking district boundaries

"And so we consumma
1949, when we merged wit
Company of Freeport. Th

ably." Mr
assets up
It was qui

"Freepo
communit
natural on
to 1905, I
could be
credit fina

"The co
a natural
island dov
Brook, an
expanded
on both si

In Marc
its second
Bank.

"Since
grown fro
happy, en
take part
ployees' c

The ma
says, "Sol
relations.
nition of
strongest

How de
If your
qualifies,
try's 14,c
Meadow
dred milli
men and

bank—people, in other words, who know Gus Weller personally or by reputation. Or do you gauge success by service rendered? Meadow Brook gives close, personal service to more than a quarter million people.

There are the checking-account customers. There are the consumer-credit customers. Meadow Brook has helped build municipal structures and schools, handling local bond issues. It has financed the building and buying of homes. It finances inventories for merchants and individual retail sales of that merchandise. In short, it is in every phase of Long Island's economy.

Today it would be difficult to find a Long Islander who is not familiar with "Mr. Meadow Brook," a friendly little character who appears in all the bank's advertising. The years of wisdom are upon him, but he remains young in spirit. The words attributed to him have the ring of sincerity.

"Mr. Meadow Brook" was created to bridge a gap. With the expansion of the bank, President Weller realized that it could no longer maintain the close personal relationship with customers that had characterized it during the early years. The little, friendly caricature was born—mothered by necessity, fathered by a realization of what he must be and do.

Is he a caricature of Gus Weller? Many people think so. To them, "Mr. Meadow Brook" and Mr. Weller are each other's alter ego. It is a sincere compliment to the man who took the job of president because he thought it was "soft"—then, without a banking background, showed other bankers how personal trust and interest in customers could create a solid success.

5. THE SEARCH FOR UNDERLYING CAUSES

Arnold Bernhard of Value Line Investment Survey

YOU KNOW THE STORY OF THE FIVE BLIND MEN WHO INSPECTED an elephant and reported their impressions. One felt the elephant's leg and said the elephant was like a tree; the second felt its tail and said it was really a rope; the third felt the animal's side and maintained that the beast was a wall; the fourth gained his impression from the ear and said it was a huge leaf; and the last felt the elephant's trunk and defended his impression that it was really a snake.

The stock market has been examined by many times five investigators who have reported equally incomplete impressions. As a result, there exists a multitude of unrelated observations reflected by an equally crosshatched picture of the stock market in the public's mind. Nevertheless, a period of unequaled prosperity, starting about the time of World War II, has led an increasing number of Americans into investing.

The majority of people who have been thus led into the market have been exposed to the name Value Line Investment Survey—a name well established in the minds of more experienced investors. The name is synonymous with Arnold Bernhard and Company, as it should be, for the Value Line method of stock analysis and evaluation is the creation of one man, Arnold Bernhard.

The president of the company sits behind a massive desk in an impressive office on the top floor of his own building in the heart of New York's Grand Central area. He lives in a beautiful home on spacious, well-tended grounds in fashionable Westport, Connecticut, fifty miles from his office. The cloak of real estate could easily give the impression that Arnold Bernhard was born on the pinnacle of success, but the actual story is more interesting than the impression promises.

After attending military school, which he disliked, young Bernhard was pleased when he could enter Williams College. "I went with three dollars and came out with six," he recalls. "I majored in English literature and never had any intention of getting into the security business while I was in college.

"After college I was in newspaper work, holding down three jobs at once. I covered the theater for *Time;* Broadway, movies, and night clubs for the New York *Post;* and syndicated my own column. The Newark *Evening News* and five or six other papers bought the column. It was a busy schedule.

"I was courting my wife then. We had met in high school years before in Rutherford, New Jersey. She had gone to Skidmore, and was teaching English in Pelham High School, a few miles north of New York City. When she came to New York, we'd go to a night club as guests, then on to the theater to a play I was to review, then to another night club I was going to report on in either the *Post* or my column."

It was an unusual training ground for a man who has become one of the country's outstanding security analysts—a man who has been able to raise a periodic hue and cry on Wall Street with his unorthodox words.

Despite the grueling pace he had set for himself, Arnold Bernhard found time to read—books on the Napoleonic era, which remains one of his hobbies; books on the stock market, which fascinated him. The *Book of Daniel Drew, Jubilee Jim Fisk,* and Jesse Livermore's *Reminiscences of a Stock Market Broker* fired his interest.

It is here that a particular trait of Arnold Bernhard's mind began to play a truly important part in shaping his future career. As long as he can remember, he has been interested in finding basic rules that determine a pattern of events. Without mathematical training, his mind nevertheless worked like the mind of a mathematician. As he read the works of acknowledged masters of the stock market, he was amazed to find that there was no formula—not, at least, in any of their books—by which to determine whether stock prices were overvalued or undervalued.

By coincidence, a friend told young Arnold of a job opening with Jesse Livermore at the time when his interest in the man was at its highest. "I got the job and was able to observe Jesse Livermore at close range," says Arnold Bernhard. "I was really amazed to find that the man handled his stock market dealings by intuition rather than by a set of rules.

"I felt that there had to be a known formula for determining the time to buy and the time to sell stock, so I decided to leave that job and look for the answer elsewhere. I had roomed with Ernest Moody at college, but I didn't want to ask him for a job. Instead, I called Moody's—who were the best-known analysts in the business—and made an appointment to see Walter Hahn, their railroad specialist.

"The subway was delayed. I was late reaching the building that Moody's was in in those days. I was running to make up for lost time, and ran right into a man as I passed through the revolving door. Of course I apologized, but he wasn't very happy about being knocked flat. And of course the man I ran into had to be Walter Hahn!

"It wasn't the best introduction in the world, but he was very nice about it, and he is still a good friend of mine.

"I was with Moody's for three years. They had been in business a long time and had their own way of doing things. I had ideas—ideas on practically everything, and I must have been a thorn in their side because I wanted everything I thought of executed at once.

"Well, of course they were not going to change their ways and methods just because a young employee thought they should. I got out. I got out and started my own business with three or four accounts.

"In the early days I did all my own research, printed the service on my own offset printing machine, folded the paper, stuffed it in envelopes, sealed and mailed the completed job. I did my own sales-promotion work.

"But that's getting ahead of the story. In the very beginning after I left Moody's, I handled individual investment accounts. After about three years my investment-counseling work reached the point where I could no longer handle it alone.

"I was managing all the accounts and studying all the securities in each of the portfolios. I thought again that there must be some method to determine when stocks were high or low, when they were good or bad values.

"The same with bonds," continues Mr. Bernhard, leading up to one of the crucial turning points in his career. "There was a greater opportunity in bonds then, in the early 1930's.

"Despite the headlines of those depression days, I could not see how the utilities were in jeopardy. So at the height of the T. V. A. scare I wrote a piece called 'Water, Water Every-where and All the Bonds Did Shrink.' It got a laugh on Wall Street and helped establish me as an expert on second-class bonds. Those are bonds not so well secured as first-class bonds; they're more speculative. There aren't many of them around any more, but they were the basis for my first real bit of success."

Today, the publisher of the Value Line Investment Survey holds an interest in only one company outside his own. It is a policy adopted to keep his opinion impartial. For the same reason, he will not serve on a board of directors.

In the early days of his investment-survey business, however, he felt free to dabble in the bond market. Arnold Bernhard understood the second-class bonds more thoroughly than the others, so naturally he bought that type, among them a number of Baldwin Locomotive Company 6 per cent bonds. His own purchase was insignificant, however, compared with the Baldwin purchases he had made for his clients.

"I bought a rather large position for them," he remembers. "You can imagine that I was horrified when Baldwin declared very shortly after that that they were going into bankruptcy. The reason they gave was that they lacked $350,000 to meet their sinking fund on bonds, even though they had a working capital of $5,000,000.

"I wrote to all Baldwin bondholders and said that there was no reason for the bonds to be down. If they would give me their support, I was going to get them one hundred cents on the dollar or bust.

"I soon had the proxies and power of attorney to represent them from a large following. Imagine me, only a kid, with a following in this matter larger than Morgan's!

"The result was a lot of experience. I became a voting trustee, a director, and, later on, a member of the executive committee of the company. I was on that for ten years during and after the reorganization."

The other company that Bernhard is connected with today is Vermont's Esty Organ Company. He is acting president. If past performance is indicative of future accomplishments, he will find the means by which to return Esty to a solid position.

While he served on Baldwin Locomotive's executive committee, his own business increased. Intelligent sales promotion added subscribers to the Value Line Investment Survey mailing lists; sound market analysis and projection held them.

How does a person, whose schooling pointed more toward his early career in newspaper work than his later career, devise a sound method of analysis and projection? The actual details —what you might call producing the product—involve complicated mathematical formulas today, but even the greatest mathematician must have a basis on which to work in solving a problem. Omitting the actual details involved in "producing the product," the method by which Bernhard decided how to proceed toward finding a pattern of stock values is an interesting case of thinking and reasoning.

If you wanted to launch an undertaking such as the Value Line Survey, it would be normal to look to the acknowledged masters of stock trading for guiding words of wisdom. Here are two examples of what you would find from two of the brightest stars in the market firmament: J. P. Morgan—"The market will fluctuate." Baron Rothschild—"I made money by buying cheap and selling dear." Both great men seem to have been guided more by the intuition Arnold Bernhard had observed in Jesse Livermore than by any established rules.

"The problem, reduced to its simplest terms," says Mr. Bernhard, "was to find a rule to guide in determining whether stocks were too high or too low. I started with a feeling that stock prices are a reflection of their earnings and dividends. At least it was a logical thing to plot earnings and dividends and prices, and see where there was a correlation.

"In effect, that is what our whole service is based on. Today we are constantly at work investigating new formulas. In 1935 I had to work it out by myself.

"First I worked with a ten-year history of the stocks I was surveying. I multiplied a stock's earnings, added it to a percentage of the book value, and found a close correlation, for the years '29 through '39, between earnings, as I multiplied them, and prices. When the war came, that method didn't work for a few years.

"Continuing to experiment with other methods of determining true values, I found that stock prices on a test period longer than I had been using showed a stronger correlation to dividends than to earnings. There were exceptions. In some cases there were no dividends, so prices had to be correlated to the company's earnings. In such cases, you see, the market price of the stock responds to earning power.

"At any rate, two variables had to correlate to the stock price. When they did that, I got into a new mathematical method somewhat different from the one I had been using. The new method requires correlation analysis."

Arnold Bernhard talks in a way that indicates he has a clear, objective grasp of his business in detail. He has had to learn to delegate responsibility—a detail which has proved too difficult for some potentially successful men to manage—and the flourishing growth of Arnold Bernhard and Company indicates that he has chosen his lieutenants and associates skillfully. The company's business now includes managing its own open-end mutual-investment fund. When the fund was offered on the market, it was—almost immediately—oversubscribed 100 per cent!

A few years ago it was said of a national political figure that nobody liked him but the voters. It's not far from wrong to paraphrase that and apply it to Arnold Bernhard—"Nobody likes him but the customers." His iconoclastic attitude toward methods of analysis less scientific than his own has set him apart from the great majority of security analysts, reporters, and forecasters.

Not long ago an Arnold Bernhard employee applied for membership in the New York Society of Security Analysts. His application was denied. "Apparently Mr. Bernhard doesn't think there is any security analysis being done by us. You presumably wouldn't want to join this organization, since we're not security analysts!" The tone was sarcastic, but Bernhard agrees with the words. His one-man stand against usual methods of security analysis came boldly to the front not long ago when Walter Winchell used space in his column to give stock predictions.

Arnold Bernhard ran an advertisement in the New York Times. Its headline was "Winchell versus Wall Street." The author of the advertisement says, "In it I said that Winchell wasn't doing anything that Wall Street wasn't doing all the time. He was giving news and the news was usually accurate. The only trouble with it was that it was not related to the price of the stock he mentioned through any formula of evaluation.

"Winchell would say that a certain person was going to bring in an oil well the following week, and the stock would jump up five points. Well, why? Maybe the stock price was already too high on the basis of the earnings that could be produced by two oil wells, but he didn't go into that. All he did was give you a piece of spot news, and the implication was that the price would do something, but there was no attempt to evaluate.

"I went on to say that's what Wall Street does. I cited about ten different cases of typical market letters where that's exactly what they do. They were furious at me. That's when one of my analysts was refused membership in the society."

Bernhard's search for underlying patterns is helped by an incisive eye. He seeks, he finds, and, for the benefit of his service's subscribers, he reports. His reports take two forms. There are the solidly packed reports that accompany the Value Line charts. Second, there are fortnightly commentaries that dig under and around a topic. They reveal the incisive mind. They reveal, too, Arnold Bernhard's background of English, reading, and journalism. There is style in the writing, and the display of a rare ability to knock out fuzzy popular opinions with the ease of a trained boxer leveling a flabby giant.

Here is an example, from *Fact and Fancy*, published June 21, 1943, of the way style can answer questioning without becoming argumentative or carping. "... There seems to be, unfortunately, a very human tendency on the part of most people to assume that if a stock's price stands some distance away from its Rating of normal value, there must be something wrong with the Value Line Rating. As soon as this very human assumption takes hold, however, the bars are down. Facts go out the window and the witch of fancy rides off on her broomstick to make sweeping discounts of the future. The devilish thing about her voyaging fancies is that they always have a little truth in them. But it is so little, and so far away. And the lost facts are so big and so near."

The subject of the *Fact and Fancy* newsletter was a comparison of Coca-Cola and Aluminum Company of America stocks. Remember the date—June 1943. We were in the midst of World War II. Opinions, along with patriotism, were at a high pitch. Here is what Arnold Bernhard and Company had to say about the two stocks. It is a good example of style, evaluation, and prediction.

"Obviously, American soldiers are carrying Coca-Cola to the far corners of the earth. Black, brown, and yellow men, by the hundreds of millions, will soon know the pause that refreshes. Sales and profits will multiply. These are the basic facts on which the discount rests. But these fancies are wraiths. Even if granted, they prove nothing. Perhaps the day will come when no cannibal would think of roasting a neighbor, unless he had a case of Coca-Cola on hand to wash him down. But when the cannibals are able to pay nickels for Coca-Cola, Africa will have been industrialized. If the Dark Continent of Africa is industrialized, more aluminum will be consumed in the process, at least for a decade or two, than Coca-Cola. And the aluminum would be sold even if the cannibals decided that they prefer their customary coconut milk to American pop. Yet the price of Coca-Cola discounts only the pleasantest fantasies, while the price of Aluminum Company common stock is determined by the most unpleasant fancies. It reflects neither the current earnings nor the happy postwar prosperity that rejoices the Coca-Cola stockholder. For Aluminum Company is a 'war' stock. . . ."

Further along the commentary compares Wrigley and Bendix in similar vein. The recommendations were to sell Coca-Cola and Wrigley to buy Alcoa and Bendix. There is ample proof, of course, that the recommendations were absolutely right.

The ability of the Value Line Survey's president to turn a phrase is evident in his remark that "the market is held in esteem somewhat like that accorded the wife in one of Chaucer's tales—too beautiful to be sure of, but nobody would have her otherwise."

The Balance of Terror, the commentary dated April 12, 1954, opens with these two paragraphs—as smoothly turned as the casing on two sticks of dynamite:

"Two heavy fears are settling down upon America: the fear of the Thermonuclear Holocaust, the possible survivor of which could only be that Power which fired first; the fear of The Inquisition, with its unknown informers and unseen accusers, its secret police files, and its investigating committees.

"Because the fear of The Holocaust is greater than the fear of The Inquisition, we write while it is still possible to do so to express the doubt that many Americans who are not foreign-policy experts must feel—the doubt whether our country's foreign policy, as recently enunciated by Secretary Dulles with the approval of the President, is morally tenable."

The biweekly newsletters range far and wide in their topics. National political moves and international events are interpreted in relation to their effect upon the stock market. The significance of inflation in France (January 1941), *Intervention in Greece* (March 1947) or *Partition of Israel and Loss of the Middle East* (February 1956) is either that of a barometer reflecting opinion or a storm affecting opinion which will, in turn, and in either case, affect the market.

Looked at another way, Arnold Bernhard's interest in the political scene is closely allied to his continuing interest in testing formulas that may provide better gauges than his present method of correlation analysis. His position is that of the cool, objective observer—a position most of us would find difficult to maintain with our established views on certain races, nations, issues, and political parties. But the man who searches for underlying causes and a repetition of historic patterns in actions and reactions must train himself to objectivity.

Arnold Bernhard has undoubtely "arrived," but the mind that sought for years to establish rules and find patterns is not ready to rest on its laurels. You can almost see how the gears of his mind mesh and turn as he discusses his business:

"Ever since adopting our method of correlative analysis, we have been groping for the best correlated variables, such as earnings and dividends, interest rates, taxes, and other things. This is a continuing search for the best variables that can be found to determine the level of prices for a period of twenty years.

"If earnings fluctuate, you expect prices to fluctuate. Prices generally fluctuate more than earnings. The point is—to find when prices fluctuate more than they should in relation to earnings and dividends. That is correlative analysis.

"Our variables are book values, earnings and dividends. We correlate these to the price. More recently we have included general stock yields as another variable, and most recently we have been experimenting with cross-sectional correlation. That means applying one stock price-earnings ratio to a large group of stocks. We may adopt the method.

"We experiment continually. Ten people on my staff do nothing but test ideas. We've tested thousands of equations. We've tried hundreds of formulas—combinations of equations —against hundreds of stocks. Thousands of correlative analysis methods. Leave out the war years. Put in the war years. Abnormal periods out. Abnormal periods in. This is all to see which will give us the most reasonable results.

"I don't think we have the final answer yet, but I feel that we have something better than—well, better than Morgan's remark that 'the stock market will fluctuate.' "

One of the oldest and most esteemed maxims of Wall Street

is that a stock is worth ten times its earnings. Iconoclast Bernhard swings his thoughtful, analytical ax on that, too. "Ten times earnings just means nothing," he says. "Each stock has its own price-dividend ratio, but the ratio changes at various levels of earning power *of the individual stock.* So you get a complicated relationship which cannot be kept in the mind, but can be traced out statistically and recorded."

Further along in his explanation of how his business operates, Value Line's president simultaneously gives another example of how his restless, questioning mind works:

"Say a stock normally sells at the old rule-of-thumb price—ten times earnings—and has for ten years in a row. If the estimated earnings for the next year are $3.00 per share, we would say that the normal price of the stock is $30.00. But if the stock is selling for $50.00 a share, one of two things is true: either earnings for the next year will be $5.00, or the market is valuing the stock at a far higher ratio than it normally does.

"Well, then, if the market values the stock higher, one of two things is true: we are in a new era of evaluation, or the market will correct itself.

"Changes in the price-earnings ratio are very slow. When the price changes radically in relation to earnings, we assume that it has deviated from the norm."

Reading between the lines of those remarks of Arnold Bernhard's reveals that, although the man is ready to do battle with the established order, he advances cautiously. There is nothing dogmatic in his approach. "One of two things is true," he says, and if there were a possibility of a third explanation, you can be sure that he would say, "One of three things." The man's caution is the sort that results from careful thought; it has nothing to do with timidity. On the contrary, Arnold Bernhard and Company is the vanguard of pioneers in the field of long-range estimating of stock earnings and dividends.

"Other stock analysts," says Bernhard, "would not make specific estimates. Say a stock was earning $10.00. If the analyst was an optimist, he would say that the stock was worth $150. If he were pessimistic, he would say that it is worth $50. The optimist would say, 'Earnings are $10.00 now, but in a few years will be $12.00 or $15.00.' The pessimist would say, 'In a couple of years earnings will be down to $6.00.' "

Bernhard has made strides in removing the elements of personal opinion or attitude. As he says, "We have gone into making all our estimates on two bases: twelve months ahead; then, under a hypothesis regarding the general economic environment, three to five years ahead.

"We don't know what is going to happen three to five years ahead, and don't try to forecast it. What we do say is that if national income grows in relation to the population—if there is no great unemployment—if commodity prices remain the same —if taxes remain the same, then national income would be $470,000,000,000 in all probability during the *average* of the three years 1959 through '61.

"If national income is up, then General Motors will probably sell so many cars—earn so much money—pay such and such dividends, and then General Motors stock, according to our estimate, would be worth so much per share.

"We may be wrong and people may disagree, but at least they know what it is we are basing our estimate on.

"Say we estimate that a stock will earn $10.00 and pay $6.00 and the price will be $100. The price will be ten times earnings and the yield 6 per cent, in accordance with past norms adjusted for trends. Someone else may say, 'It's not going to be that way, it's going to be some other way.' All well and good. At least he knows what he is disagreeing with! Let him come up with a better estimate, based on a better formula of known factors and variables."

Reports and estimates drawn up by Bernhard Company analysts are carefully reviewed. Their forecasts, estimates, or implications are checked against actual trends and developments. There is the compensation of fatter salary checks for those who make the grade by proving their worth in this field of mental gymnastics.

Arnold Bernhard's principal frustration—he can't find a formula to beat it!—is the number of unread books in his library. Many of them are studies of Lord Nelson, his particular hero of the Napoleonic era. His average workday is twelve hours long, leaving little time for the reading he plans to resume "when things get easier"—which will be after he reorganizes the Esty Organ Company and installs a president to take over the reins he is holding.

There is a tennis court behind the Bernhards' Westport home "with a machine to sling balls at me if I can't find a partner. Talk about the market; that machine simply can't be beaten!

"My wife and I are interested in the Connecticut Symphony. She's an officer. I think I am, too, but I'm not sure. I did a lot locally for a while but had to give it up. I was president and a director of the YMCA. On the board of the hospital for a while. And I headed up the Building Committee of the Congregational Church at the time we moved it across the Boston Post Road to where it stands now. Maybe you read about it in *Life*. It was quite an undertaking.

"When the business in Vermont is settled, I hope to get back to playwriting—seriously. That and reading."

It sounds entirely like hobby time, but even in his hobby of studying Napoleonic times, Arnold Bernhard finds rules and patterns—the rules and patterns that develop from life under a given set of circumstances. Looking under the surface of bright uniforms, horse-drawn coaches, and slow communications systems, Bernhard says, "Those days were quite like our own. Subversive movements were sweeping Europe at that time, backed up by an imperialistic force. There were heretical notions regarding the monarchy and the established order of things. There are many similarities between then and now."

The man whose urge to find an underlying pattern by which to establish rules that would produce estimates of reasonable accuracy can use his urge in his hobbies as well as his work. Undoubtedly, other fields than stock analysis would yield up dividends to a man who could stick to finding the patterns and rules with the tenacity and determination of Arnold Bernhard.

6. ONE JUMP AHEAD—
TO SUCCESS

Jack Spound of the Charlton Company

JACK SPOUND WAS BORN TO THRIVE ON APPARENTLY BAD OMENS.
If there was a single good omen, it was the date of his birth—
George Washington's Birthday, 1893. His hard-working immigrant parents well fitted the industrious scheme of things in
Chelsea, Massachusetts, but even the father's skill as an upholsterer—which had been the trade of his father before him—
could do no more than provide the bare necessities of life.

There was family life, but little besides. Jack Spound's
parents were middle-aged when he appeared on the scene. The
usual joy in having a son was entirely too well balanced by
the burden of supporting him.

Jack was eight when he began contributing to the family's
finances. He rose when it was still dark to be among the first
venders of morning papers. He got his own breakfast, and
got it quietly so as not to disturb his mother, whose delicate
health called for rest. An hour later his catlike silence vanished
as Jack proclaimed, "Papers, papers—get your *Globe Journal
and Post*" in a tone that rose above most of his competitors.
Scott and Shackleton discovered King Edward Land in Antarctica; the Pan-American Exposition was in the newspapers
for six months; Marconi signaled the letter "S" across the Atlantic; Leon Czolgosz assassinated President McKinley—but the
big news to eight-year-old Jack Spound was that he was contributing a few dollars a week to the family.

Newspaper hawking, and its varying income, is for boys. At the age of fourteen, Jack took on a man's job, becoming a wage earner in a shoe factory. Hours were long, the work hard and tedious in 1907, the year the United States knew financial panic. The young giant twentieth century had yet to develop even the first faint visible signs of job or income security. It was a tough age.

Jack had quit his schooling while in the eighth grade. His mingling with older men in the shoe factory began to impress on him the difference between his educated and uneducated elders. By a simple process of selection, he chose to raise his own level of education. It was a firm determination, but at the time Jack made the decision there were no means by which to implement it.

However, determination seems to have been a family characteristic. Dora Spound, now invalided, announced her strong wish that Jack follow in the footsteps of his father and grandfather. There were long discussions under the muted glow of a kerosene lamp. Jack weighed two years' experience in the shoe factory against his mother's wish, weighed it against the advantage of becoming closer to his father through the interest of mutual work, and left the factory to become an upholsterer.

That decision, like all of Jack's decisions, was made carefully and with reason. One of the elements dictating his change of jobs was the fact that he would find it a little easier to commute to Boston evenings to pick up his education.

At the YMCA, Spound studied mathematics, English, French, and the subject which held his interest most strongly—philosophy. Dog-eared volumes by Spencer and Spinoza are still on his library shelves, nestled among newer books, their pages marked with definitions and comments written by young Jack in 1910.

Is the zealous study of philosophy a building block in constructing a furniture company? If you take the Charlton Company's successful, quiet, energetic president as your clinical example, the answer is an unqualified Yes. Along with the old study-class volumes of philosophy, Spound has brought philosophy itself right along with him. Nor has he found it necessary to twist the old verities to fit his attitude toward life. "Treat a man right and he will treat you right" might be called Spound's rephrasing of an older idea that had to do with casting one's bread upon the waters. His belief that a man can accomplish whatever he sets out to do is rooted in a firm soil of philosophy, not pride.

The upholsterer son of immigrant parents, the former newsboy of interrupted educational background, enlisted in the Signal Corps. His mental abilities were recognized—attested to by the fact that the Army sent him to the University of Vermont to study the new science of wireless telegraphy. Jack was in the unit in Rockport, Massachusetts that first carried on transatlantic wireless communication.

For many, rubbing against the new science was to change their lives. To Spound, it was an interesting interruption. After the war he returned to Boston and to upholstering.

The mental agility that had tagged the soldier for special instruction at the University of Vermont marked the returned civilian. He rose from workbench to a foreman's job in the Boston furniture factory.

A girl who had taught school in Perth Amboy, New Jersey, caught Jack's eye. Their early courtship had one fairly serious drawback. Rose, having graduated from Teachers College and taught school herself, held Jack's lack of formal education against him. And again his mental agility came to the fore as he displayed a wide knowledge of current events, astronomy (a useful subject on starry nights!), economics, and philosophy. A practicing part of that philosophy, too, was Spound's belief that a man can accomplish whatever he sets his heart to—and in this case he had set his heart on marriage. The wedding took place in 1921.

Eight years later Plant Manager Spound was in a strong, enviable economic position. He was well regarded by both management and the men under him. His family—there were two children, Marcia and Albert—was well housed. The future looked bright. There was money in the bank, a sound life-insurance program, and—"like everybody else"—stock bought on margin with the idea of keeping income up to spiraling values and costs. These were adjuncts to a sound, secure position.

November 1929 dealt its never-to-be-forgotten blow to the stock market. Jack Spound was caught up in the economic whirlwind that followed. Pleading calls from his broker sent Spound to the savings bank. Joseph, the third child, was born in January, three months after the crash. Throughout 1930 Spound went back and back again to cover his stock, until the savings account was gone. He turned to the insurance company, borrowed on his policies up to their full loan value. Nineteen thirty withered away, his finances withering with it. Nineteen thirty-one promised little, then took away even that— Jack's employer went bankrupt. His seniority, his investment in the firm, his job—everything was gone with the inexplicable sudden finality that drove men to frustrated tears, insanity, and suicide. An economic river had evaporated overnight, leaving only the dry sand of bread lines and discouragement.

The men who had gone to France to save the world for democracy took to selling apples on street corners. Charitable organizations linked arms with governmental welfare agencies, spread a dollar as far as it would go, and saw the ranks of the needy increase. Men raked leaves for the government.

It was not a fertile year in which to plant the seed of a new company. Families were "shrinking"—doubling up. Children moved in with parents, or parents with children. Who would think of starting—of all things—a furniture company in the face of that fact? Jack Spound thought of it. As with all his major decisions, he spent a long time thinking about it.

He talked over a plan with some of the former workers in the bankrupt Boston factory. Yes, idleness had them itchy, too. Yes, they would pool a few dollars to capitalize a new furniture company with Jack Spound at the helm.

The single hardest moment in starting the new enterprise came when the new president performed the act that gave him the money he needed for his capital interest. He pawned his wife's engagement ring for $400.

The new company opened shop on Charlton Street in Everett, Massachusetts, a suburb of Boston. It opened with its limited capital invested principally in rent, a sewing machine, a few tools and benches, fabric, upholstery filling, and furniture frames purchased from an outside source. It opened with one other asset—the reputation Jack Spound had established during his years as foreman and manager in his previous employer's plant. That reputation was equivalent to a high credit rating among suppliers; the philosophy Jack Spound had brought with him from the YMCA classes could be seen translated into inventory far greater than the young Charlton Company's receivables.

Jack could have added "of all trades" to his name. He sold on the road. He supervised production, speeding it up wherever possible to convert raw materials into money.

It became commonplace for the president—the title must have seemed a huge joke in those days—to follow the delivery truck to a retail store. Upon receipted delivery of the furniture, he would wait for a check, receipt the bill, then dash across town to the company's bank to cover the pay roll. Several times the need for speed brought a calling down from policemen, but only once was a cop so barren of the milk of human kindness that Spound was late for the bank.

Enterprise, energy, and faith in the outcome formed the practical and philosophical basis of the Charlton Company. Little by little—imperceptibly at first—it gained a toehold among furniture retailers, then slowly secured a broader and

firmer foothold. It outgrew the Everett location and moved to
Fitchburg, Massachusetts. There the upholsterers and finishers
shared space in a building with the makers of luggage, bottle
caps, and spaghetti.

The move was made during the middle thirties, when college
graduates jumped at the chance to become movie ushers. If
the bread lines were shorter, government-project pay rolls were
longer. If there was less despair, it was principally because we
had learned to live with a depression. Yet into this bleak period
Jack Spound read opportunity and challenge.

The need for families to "double up" still existed. Then why
not, Spound reasoned, furniture that will do a double job for
them? If living quarters must serve two purposes, why not
furniture that serves two purposes?

"If I could give those people something they could afford
that they could use for a living room in the daytime and that
would also be comfortable as a bed," Mr. Spound recalls, "then
I figured I would have a market and we would have a business."

The sofa bed had been around for years. Charlton spent
countless days and nights and many precious dollars to develop and perfect it according to Jack Spound's vision. Charlton improved and simplified the mechanical operation—gave
it the extra durability required for 'round-the-clock usage—introduced a fresh variety of handsomely proportioned styles in
both modern and Early American styles.

As the 1930's drew to a close, the company from which
Charlton was renting the Fitchburg property wanted to sell
the building. Their action in the case is as firm a tribute to
Jack Spound's reputation as any that can be found. They offered
the building to him, naming a reasonable figure.

"I would like to buy it. I think I could fill it soon," Spound
told them, "but I just don't have the money for the down
payment."

"Then we will lend you the money to make the down payment."

Faith in a businessman's ability and integrity rarely reaches that pinnacle of expression.

Expansion of sales and production facilities followed the purchase of the building. World War II saw the company retrench, its facilities not being adaptable to war work, but immediately after the end of hostilities, it double-timed to take up the slack that had grown between supply and demand.

Charlton Company entered a period of rebirth. The period was entirely different from the first years. Our economy expanded. Homes and apartment houses sprang up. Families no longer considered "doubling up." But another change had taken place. The building dollar had shrunk in value, and the size of dwelling units with it. Convertible furniture was as much a necessity then as it had been when Charlton turned out its first two-purpose sofa bed.

An ingenious conveyor system was installed in Fitchburg. Hooks ran on overhead conveyors from department to department, doubling the productive value of the factory's floor space.

Outgrowing even the modernized plant, Charlton opened a second factory in nearby Leominster. It stands as the most efficient furniture manufacturing plant in the country today. Facilities minimize the demands on human labor. An electric oven "cures" the bonding resin holding matched slats of wood together. In sixty seconds the bond is stronger than the New England hardwood itself. Saws, sanders, multiple-headed drills, hydraulic ovens that laminate the wood plies they curve—all are geared to the productive capacities of one another.

The nationally known furniture company is a fairly recent innovation in America. Traditionally it has been a regional business, a "small" business that could be started with limited capital. Today, that is changing—and Charlton is changing with it. In 1952 a third Charlton factory was opened in Los Angeles to supply the fourteen western states. The company's products are sold throughout the United States. More branches are being considered.

The California plant is directed by Albert Spound, Jack's older son, who is also responsible for styling and product development. He has been busy on both jobs. The California plant hums. In addition, the Charlton line of furniture has grown beyond the complete groups of convertibles available in modern and maple to include chairs that rock, recline, and swivel. Chairs in many styles. "Furniture that does something."

Morris Loeb, Jack's son-in-law, has developed an efficient national sales organization. Joseph Spound—the depression baby —has the triple job of heading up production in the New England plants, labor relations, and coordination between all branches of the company.

Jack Spound still begins his day at 7 A.M. His organization is efficient and well staffed with capable executives, but the dynamic spark of twenty-five years ago is still there, driving the company toward new achievements.

By any standard, and especially by contrast to its early days, the Charlton Company of today is vast, intricate, complex. Three plants. Wholesale showrooms in many large cities. Dealers from coast to coast. It is a story of achievement, but company thinking is not concerned with what has been achieved, it centers around the challenges of the future. The new branches under consideration are already being mapped out. Radically different products are being developed and launched to maintain Charlton's leadership in the fast-growing field of convertible furniture.

Recently the company began production of the first—and so far, only—all-electric, fully automatic convertible sofa bed. Charlton's feeling toward the push-button sofa bed invented and designed by Albert Spound is that it marks a turning point in the field of living-room furniture. A few major manufacturers have introduced appliances that resemble furniture;

Charlton has introduced furniture that plugs in like an appliance.

Still another Charlton frontier today is in the field of automation. At this writing the company has most recently installed the first fully automatic and fully conveyorized rough-cut lumber mill in the United States. An outstanding feature of the mill is its intricate series of conveyors. They automatically carry the lumber from one machine to another in the proper time cycle, bringing about a marked increase in production at substantially lowered cost.

For the first time in furniture-making history, waste lumber is carried away from the production machinery—again by a process that is fully automatic—by a series of conveyor belts located under the floor. The belts lead directly to the boiler room and the fires that heat the drying kilns. As an example of ingenious economy and waste disposal it ranks with the practice of other New Englanders a hundred years ago—the Yankee whalers who used boiled "horse pieces" of whale blubber in their fires to "try out" successive vats of the oil-rich flesh.

Charlton has not sat still, nor will it. Further advances in automation are in the offing to increase efficiency and total production. Where hand workmanship is essential, it will remain.

There is little free time in the daily activity of Jack Spound, still the dynamic spark of the firm. Not long ago the vice-president of a large engineering firm remarked, "No company, no matter how large and powerful, could ever buy the talent and energy which Mr. Spound gives to this company. The energy expresses itself in a full workday—guiding company policies, supervising, in conference, or on the production floor itself."

Active? Yes. Yet the significant and unique fact about this man's life is not how hard he works or the success he has achieved, but rather its shining example of how a man lives by a philosophy.

Jack Spound has a philosophy of quiet confidence in the attainability of positive goals. Catch him in a reflective mood and he will carefully explain that "the man who sets himself a goal can achieve that goal if he holds fast with unshakable faith." Are they just so many nice-sounding words? Not at all. He has proved his philosophy time and again—proved it so convincingly that he has inspired many around him to live by the same principles.

7. VALUES AND VISION

Victor W. Farris of Farris Engineering

ONE OF THE MOST SERIOUS SINGLE BOTTLENECKS IN OUR WORLD War II Navy and Merchant Marine expansion program was smashed by thirty-one-year-old engineer-inventor Victor W. Farris. The bottleneck was safety-valve production. His answer was simple, straightforward, and fast.

The young engineer, who today has more than seventy patents to his credit and twice that number pending in Washington, wanted to join the Navy. An ardent boat enthusiast and a member of the United States Power Squadron, Farris was acquainted with small-boat handling, rules of the road, seamanship and navigation—he had the qualities as well as the desire to become a valuable Navy officer. "You're a lot more valuable to us where you are," he was told by a friend, a high-ranking naval officer.

Vic Farris at that particular moment was in the position of general manager for a manufacturer of regulating valves. "We make 'em today," he says, "but they are really the 'Model T' of the valve industry."

Working as a consultant in addition to his general managership, Farris was instrumental in the designing of the heat-balance system for the Liberty Ships of World War II. In the course of doing that job, he was startled by the safety-valve bottleneck that threatened to scuttle America's maritime expansion needs. The country's two great valve manufacturers were swamped with orders. Swing shifts and long work weeks were unable to cope with the demand.

Victor Farris jumped into the middle of the problem to organize his own company. He had three employees, a bench in the rear of a silk printing plant suffering a wartime lapse, and a lot of energy. A week later he had a telephone, printed stationery—and $45,000 in government orders. Sharp dealing? Not at all. Victor Farris knew exactly what he was going to do to fill those orders. He would meet government specifications for mechanical operation and safety tolerances through application of his engineering know-how and administrative ability.

Within a year the new company president had sixty firms, representing 750 people, in and around Bergen County, New Jersey, doing work for him on a subcontracting basis. Single-handed, he surveyed practically every shop, large and small, in the area. He learned what machines and man power were available, together with their production speeds, and integrated the sprawl of subcontractors into a unified producer of valve parts which were assembled, inspected, and tested in his own plant. It was less than twelve months after Mr. Farris had visited Washington in person to have the government reverse the opinion of one of its own inspectors—an inspector who said Farris Engineering had no machines, hence could not produce for the government.

A safety valve is a remote thing to "the man on the street," yet it plays a part in your life if you drive a car, ride a railroad, open a cellophane-wrapped package, drink beer, use paper, or wear clothes. Somewhere behind the scenes safety valves are in the picture, playing their part as "the last safeguard of human life." When all else fails—electricity, power, mechanical, even human hands, a safety valve will "blow off" to reduce dangerous pressures.

Because of its importance as a factor in safeguarding human life, a manufacturer cannot simply place a safety valve on the market and promote sales. The valve must pass rigid government inspections—pass all of them with a 100 per cent rating

—before the valve maker can offer his wares to industry. To put it another way, a newcomer to the field must combine engineering talent with patience, honesty of intent, sales and administrative skill. Victor Farris had that combination within him.

Leaping into the midst of the wartime safety-valve bottleneck, he broke it with a design that clearly illustrates one of his favorite maxims: "Keep it simple!" Valve housings are, traditionally, castings; the molten metal is cast to fairly close measurements and machined to close tolerances. Vic Farris multiplied production by using steel tubing, which he cut, swedged, and welded, in place of the castings. "It can't be done," he was told—which made the idea precisely the kind of challenge he likes to meet.

The president of numerous engineering corporations, six real-estate companies, a publishing company, and the Victor Farris Foundation was born in Buffalo, New York, in 1910. He was one of four boys—all destined to become prominent, although the family voted young Victor "least likely to succeed."

"I liked sports," he recalls, "but never took a scholastic honor in my life. I was interested in things that went around—gears, machines, racing cars—anything mechanical, and my marks suffered. I just skinned through the University of Buffalo and M. I. T."

Coaching less gifted athletes helped undergraduate Farris pay his way through college. It achieved a neat balance between helping him get the education he knew he should have and keeping him in the swimming pool or the gymnasium where he preferred to be.

How did the pupil who "just skinned through" become a leading industrialist? There are two answers—one simple and fairly obvious, the other difficult to phrase. To take the easier answer first: Victor Farris lives by a set of rules. Boiled down to a few words, they are: first, Keep It Simple; second, Don't

Take Yourself too Seriously; third (his company's motto),
Progress Through Honest Purpose.

And having been boiled down to a few words, the rules
appear *too* simple—even "corny" by today's standards of
sophistication. The man who has made a success of his life
through the application of those rules has found, to paraphrase
Kipling, that the gods of the copybook are stronger than the
gods of the market place.

"Keep it simple" means sticking to essential facts, whether
the problem is one of the moment or one that will affect your
entire life. Issues become difficult as they become clouded with
extraneous details. Weed out everything but the essentials;
draw a diagram or make a list of the problem's *important*
points, then tackle the problem on that basis, and the aura of
difficulty that surrounded it will disappear.

"Don't take yourself too seriously" can act in place of a
nerve tonic. If you refuse to be overly serious about yourself
and your importance, you will be *in*tense without being *tense*
—even if you are the world's largest manufacturer of safety-
relief valves for refineries, which Victor Farris is today. "I'm
not trying to prove anything to anybody," he says. "I'm just
trying to live and use whatever talents I've got. I've found
that most of the people who take themselves seriously are the
little wise guys who are out to 'show' somebody."

"Progress through honest purpose" is a mouthful in an era
that leans more toward "catchy" slogans than toward those
that require thought. You can judge the quality of the slogan
by the fact that it could be a four-word capsule history of Vic
Farris and his companies.

Numerous times—particularly when he was engaged in war
work—Farris heard subcontractors remark, "I lost money on
that last job for you." His invariable reply was, "Then refigure it and send me a new bill. I don't want you to get fat,
but I don't want you to go out of business either."

There were many subcontractors who would go out of their

way for *that* prime contractor. No one could meet the president of Farris Engineering Corporation and consider him "soft"; subcontractors whom he kept from using red ink learned that the "honest purpose" in his slogan was all-inclusive. The dishonest person, the one who grabs a fast dollar, may be around for the honeymoon but won't be around for the anniversary. Not only has Farris grown from one small factory to many, from one corporation to fourteen by practicing its own slogan, but in addition the president and other officers have never been worried about a government investigation.

Those are the rules, the principles of Victor W. Farris. The second reason—if you can call it that—for his success will have to wait on new developments in many fields of medical science before it can be fully stated. It is a possible reason which the man discusses with humility, groping for an answer in a field that will remain dark until biochemists, psychologists, endocrinologists, and researchers in related fields make many more scientific advances.

It was mentioned earlier that of the four Farris children, young Victor was conceded to be the least likely to succeed. In another family he might have accomplished an Ugly Duckling turnabout, putting his three brothers to shame by achieving the position he holds today. The fact is that all four became successful—so outstandingly successful that the new edition of the *Encyclopedia Americana* treats with the four as a group, a new departure in reference works.

Emil M. Farris, the oldest brother, is an executive of the American Viscose Corporation, in charge of their cellophane activities. He was a member of the famous Lafayette Escadrille and has flown his own plane for nearly thirty years. He was aviation editor of the Buffalo *Times* and is a member of the Quiet Birdmen. Emil Farris ran the 1952 airplane show in Philadelphia. The following year he received the Civil Aeronautics award for performing the most outstanding work in the field during the preceding twelve months.

Dr. Louis G. Farris is one of the best-known specialists in gynecology and obstetrics in New York State, with a reputation that goes far beyond its borders. He is on the American board of Obstetrics and Gynecology. He is well known for his work in planned parenthood, and highly regarded for his work in obstetrics and gynecology.

The fourth brother, Dr. Edmond J. Farris, is world famous for his books, lectures, research, and practice in the field of human fertility. If the medical profession gave decorations on the style of the military, he would wear as much "fruit salad" as a four-star combat general. His scientific research over a span of more than twenty years is the basis of the medical profession's standard work on fertility problems. Executive director of the Wistar Institute of Anatomy at Philadelphia's University of Pennsylvania, he was formerly professor of anatomy at the University of Michigan, the University of South Carolina, and the University of Buffalo. In 1949 he received the National Urological award. Dr. Edmond has lectured before medical groups in the United States, Canada, England, France, and Italy. Today, in addititon to his post at Wistar Institute, he is general director of the Farris Institute for Parenthood in Philadelphia.

"It may be genes, or it may be glandular; nobody knows," Victor Farris says, twin vertical creases in his forehead indicating that he is irked because the frontiers of knowledge have not advanced far enough to provide a reason for all four Farris brothers rising to success. "My mother was a remarkable woman. She may have passed something along to us. Some of my ancestors were in the French cabinet. An uncle was highly successful in California real estate; at one point I think he owned about half of Pasadena."

Those are the bits and scraps. Perhaps someday another Dr. Louis or Dr. Edmond will be able to fit them into a pattern.

"It might help everybody, you know," says a man who needs no help up the ladder, "if the scientists or doctors could discover what it is that makes one man progress while another just sits still. Just think of the progress we'd make."

"Progress" to Victor Farris is an all-inclusive word. It means progress in the humanities as well as in the laboratory, it includes charity as well as business, it implies advancing others as well as self.

A few years ago Dr. Edmond finished a book. The work was on the threshold of advancing medical knowledge. It was the result of many years' work. It had been accepted by a publisher. He had corrected the galley proofs. Then the publisher went bankrupt. When Victor Farris learned of the situation, he acted rapidly—he bought the publishing firm, adding Authors Press, Inc., to his list of holdings. His brother's book was published and the field of medical knowledge enriched.

Several employees have benefited by phone calls that the boss has made without their knowledge. Knowing that they needed money for a good purpose, he has urged them to visit the Palisades Trust Company, of which he is a director. While they were on their way to the bank, he has called to endorse the loans personally. Neither he nor the bank ever disclosed the fact. There exists only a verbal bond—good enough for the bank because of the person who made the bond.

Walk through the Farris factory today, and it is difficult to believe that the president had only three employees (one recruited from a delivery truck directly into the valve field), a bench, and a telephone in 1943. Production is so closely scheduled on all machines that only the most advanced methods of visual control meet the production scheduling department's requirements. Similar control methods are used to keep track of inventory.

The factory itself is equipped with modern automatic machinery supervised by men who constantly check finished items—even screws—with micrometers. A safety valve calls for precision down to the smallest detail.

Another section of the Palisades Park, New Jersey, factory

is occupied by the Farris Flexible Valve Company. Its products are as much of an innovation as the welded-steel safety valve that broke the shipbuilding bottleneck. A Farris flexible valve consists principally of a clamping device operated by a rotating handle and a length of tough, flexible hose. Turn the wheel and jaws pinch opposite walls of the tube together to regulate or stop the flow of liquid. Keep it simple? It would be hard to find a flow-control valve of simpler design, but it took Victor Farris to find it. And it is no more than a mechanical version of the way you control the flow of water through a garden hose without a nozzle, by pinching it together.

Besides mechanical perfection, improved appearance is sought after. Valve housings are cast by the lost-wax process, the same method used to cast ring mountings and other jewelry. As a result, the pitted surfaces and broken letters that characterize the more usual sand castings are replaced by smooth surfaces and highly readable letters spelling out the company name. The detail is unimportant as far as performance is concerned, but indicative of the way Vic Farris thinks about every detail of production.

A valve must be invented, engineered, "modeled up," and must pass tests of quality and performance. After that, only one question remains: Will it work? Because each valve will protect human lives, industrial equipment, or both, each one must answer that question affirmatively by passing a critical inspection test.

Farris has the highest pressure steam-testing station in its section of the country, with an operating pressure of 2,000 pounds per square inch at 1,000 degrees Fahrenheit. Testing and production equipment—much of it built by the company to meet its own specifications—is housed in four modern factory buildings in Palisades Park. In a decade the company moved three times. Each time, orders and production soared above expectations, calling for additional space and a nearly constant expansion program. The new offices are air-conditioned. There is a company cafeteria, a well-equipped clinic.

Other factory buildings in Texas produce Farris valves for the petroleum industry, cutting shipping time from a week to overnight. Farris-Pickering Regulator Company is the successor to the country's oldest manufacturer of speed regulators and governors. Farris HydroTorque Corporation manufactures valves that operate by remote control; turn one control a thousandth of an inch and a second control fifty feet away will move exactly the same distance. Farris HydroSeal Corporation manufactures hydraulic control units that prevent oil leakage; a flexible rubber sheath connected to the piston or driving device contains the oil so that not even the thinnest film can escape along the cylinder walls. These are used to operate thousands of automobile windows.

Victor Farris is a director of the Palisades Park Chamber of Commerce as well as of the Palisades Trust Company, charter president of the Lions' Club, a member of the Economic Club, the American Society for the Advancement of Science, the American Chemical Society, American Society of Mechanical Engineers, an organ society, several yacht clubs, and other groups.

It adds up to a complex list of activities for a man who says "Keep it simple." Yet it is obvious that if any one phase were permitted to become complicated, the others would become impossible.

"If I have to get in front of a microphone or a camera, or up on a stage," says Vic Farris, "I do it without getting a stomach full of butterflies. I simply approach it as another job to be done. The other way—if you let the butterflies in—you get nervous, tense, and can't do the job.

"After it's all over, I may wonder how I had the nerve to do it, but by that time it's done, so the reaction doesn't matter.

"All that tension is up in the front part of your mind," he continued, tapping his forehead. "All the worries are right there—all the untruths, the dishonesty that prevents you from keeping a job simple and solving it.

"Truth is in the subconscious. That's why I keep a pencil and notebook handy by my bed. Go to sleep and let your conscious mind relax. Your subconscious will keep working. Mine does. Very often I wake up at four in the morning and finish a drawing. All the complications are gone; just the simple truth comes through.

"One night during the war I was working on a drawing for a valve. There was a deadline to be met and I was working as hard as I could. Right in the middle of it I'll be damned if the air-raid sirens didn't go off. I finished the drawing in a closet by candlelight."

How does a man with Victor Farris's drive and energy keep his mind from bogging down? Interest in hobbies is the answer. He is a photographer, stamp collector, radio ham, golfer (shooting in the low eighties). He swims and takes delight in his sleek fifty-eight-foot ocean-going cruiser, the *Kerida*. Although he cannot read a note of music, one of his most time-consuming hobbies is playing his electric organ.

Hobbies extend themselves to Vic Farris. Not entirely satisfied with the effects he could obtain from the organ, he has installed speakers throughout his Tenafly, New Jersey, home to produce effects beyond those incorporated by the organ builder.

The other occupant of the Tenafly home is Mrs. Farris, the former Celia Lipton, a beautiful young woman of considerable reputation in England, where she starred in light opera and musical comedies. She has been seen by American audiences in *The Hunchback of Notre Dame* and other television productions.

The Farrises spend their winter vacation aboard the *Kerida* in southern waters. With his interest in hobbies, the Skipper obviously knows how to relax, but his alert mind never takes a complete vacation. The conscious interest that led to the echo chambers and added speakers for his electric organ, the interest that opens new product and sales visions for Farris when he reads a letter of inquiry, has been evident aboard the *Kerida*, too.

The cruiser's diesel engines naturally fascinate the engineer in the Skipper. How to get more horsepower out of them? It's a question that many men have asked—yachtsmen, truck-fleet operators, industrialists with diesel power in their plants.

"It's a problem that has had the hell engineered out of it. Engineers get into complicated problems of heat, air expansion, ratios, and when they get through you often find that the attachment which was supposed to give you added horsepower uses it all up, putting you right back where you started."

What is coming of that? A new Farris product—a diesel turbine kit designed to reduce fuel consumption 15 per cent and increase horsepower up to 100 per cent.

"It'll turn over dollars," says Vic Farris, "even if it doesn't mean much to the company. In the final analysis, that's what businessmen do—turn over dollars. If they don't, they're not helping anybody.

"I'm going to have someone else engineer my turbine. I'll produce and sell 'em. If you have a highly complicated problem, this isn't for you. But if you want an inexpensive unit that you can attach yourself, this will be it. You won't cut your fuel bill 90 per cent or even 50 per cent, but it will be designed to cut fuel costs a measurable 15 per cent, and it will deliver that saving."

If previous progress of the Farris corporations is any indication, the diesel fuel saver will be a nationwide success. Victor Farris is a man who rubs an idea against talent to produce a spark of production that grows to a flame of sales and employment.

What has he to say about opportunities for young men? Speaking of them, and young engineers in particular, he says,

"Don't watch the clock or the pay check. Keep your mind on the work, not the hours or the immediate reward.

"My first invention was a gadget to slip on the dashboard of Model-A Fords. They had the instruments in a little cluster. The thing I invented slipped over the dash to make it look impressive. Merely a gadget good for sales for a year or two. But the banker and businessman I worked with built up such expenses for diemaking and sales promotion that I never collected a cent in royalties."

The obvious inference is that Farris's 1934 experience with his first invention could have caused complete discouragement if he had kept his eye on the pay check instead of on the future. It is equally obvious that neither the banker nor businessman had another opportunity to do business with the rising inventor.

"And I always tell young men not to take themselves too seriously. A lot of young engineers are graduating from college right into $12,000 jobs. Companies invest that kind of money because they need a pool of engineers. The trouble is that a lot of the boys think they are worth that kind of money as soon as they get their first check. They take themselves seriously—and then heaven help them! They lose perspective."

The engineer-president who recommends disregard for pay check, working hours, and self-esteem does not do it for the sake of himself getting more for each dollar he pays in salary; that type of businessman would hardly tell his subcontractors to refigure their bills and rebill him at a higher cost. No. Victor Farris's recommendations are aimed at instilling a thought-and-work pattern that will help the individual climb his own ladder to success.

Undoubtedly the man's law-school background has been helpful in shaping the Victor Farris of today. He has the ability, sharpened through training, to categorize matters. "Keep it simple" is the keystone—and he has built fourteen corporations from that starting point. One corporation is concerned solely with real estate, another with factory buildings, a third is his patent-holding organization. These vertical business classifications make for simplicity of operation in each with a minimum of overlapping duties and departments.

Still another organization that has nothing to do with sales or production is the Victor W. Farris Foundation. It was established to aid charity and will award educational scholarships to deserving youngsters.

Victor W. Farris emerges as an individualist of the new school. Not a "rugged individualist" of the last century whose only regard was self-regard, but an educated, balanced, rational individualist who realizes and assumes responsibility for others.

Keep it simple, and don't take yourself too seriously. Who knows? Maybe you, like Victor W. Farris, will be able to summarize your career in the slogan "Progress through honest purpose."

8. IF THE SHOE FITS

William Manowitz of Hussco Shoe

WILLIAM MANOWITZ, PRESIDENT OF THE HUSSCO SHOE COMpany in Honesdale, Pennsylvania, says he started "with a dream and a bankbook."

Given these ingredients, you might say that almost anyone could achieve success. In Bill Manowitz's case, the ingredients were definitely out of proportion. The big dream was independence. The bankbook was worth exactly $350. He has built his dream into reality and parlayed his bank account into a more than $10,000,000 retail business in 1956.

Of course Manowitz had other attributes. He had an original plan coupled with aggressiveness and persistence. Linked to the dream of independence, those qualities led him from small beginnings to his present position—president of one of the nation's largest manufacturers of teen-age, women's, and children's shoes. Shoes for men are being added to round out a complete family shoe line under the Huskies brand name.

Bill Manowitz was a salesman in a retail shoestore. He learned about shoes from the customer's point of view, and he learned an interesting fact about the shoe business in general. Unlike most retail businesses, chain-store operations are secondary to independent retailers. There are 23,000 independent shoestores in the country—more than any one manufacturer could cover continually and successfully.

That fact had undoubtedly bothered shoe manufacturers long before Bill Manowitz gambled his $350 on a plan to bring a sizable percentage of them under the Huskies banner. His plan, reduced to simplest terms, was to adapt the distribution setup of the hard-lines fields to the shoe industry.

"I was told the idea was ridiculous," says the president of Hussco, "but I was ignorantly stubborn that the plan would work."

Despite the Operation Success that has risen above the foundation of distribution, no other manufacturer has been able to duplicate it. Why? Manowitz's explanation is, "It takes a great deal of patience, bluff, and perseverance."

Bluff was required in the early days of Huskies. Bill was twenty-one in 1934 when he founded his company. But even then patience and perseverance were more important elements in building sales through distribution.

"Stick with me and I'll stick with you" was the message Manowitz gave distributors. He sought out, not experienced shoe distributors, but jobbers who knew distribution patterns and methods—houses that sold boots, tennis shoes, laces, soles, heels, ornaments. Not "fat" companies content with their percentage of whatever came in, but young companies eager for profitable lines. Manowitz recognized that they could utilize their knowledge of distribution methods as effectively as any companies whose experience had been confined to shoes. The thought was revolutionary—and right.

The "stick with me and I'll stick with you" philosophy was equally revolutionary. Today Huskies remain the only national brand of shoes merchandised through distributors that guarantee sales areas. There are no direct customers, no "house accounts" short-circuiting jobbers.

One of the country's giant department stores wanted to add Huskies to its shoe department to meet increasing customer demand. Bill Manowitz visited the shoe buyer.

"We buy direct from all our suppliers," said the buyer.

"We sell only through distributors," replied Manowitz.

"That's the policy of our store," the buyer told him.

"And that's the policy of my company." Manowitz was

adamant. A large sale hung in the balance, but on the other side of the scale was Huskies' promise of guaranteed sales areas. In the end, common sense drove the department store to stock Huskies on Manowitz's conditions.

Between the day he drew his $350 from the bank and the day he was in a position to impose his business methods on a great department store Manowitz obviously had to accomplish a great deal.

The interesting method of distribution and Bill Manowitz's philosophy on markup and turnover could overshadow the basic item itself, the casual shoe.

If your memory goes back to 1934, you will recall that few women then wore moccasins. All low-heeled shoes accounted for less than a fifth of the shoes produced for girls and women. It was considered a dying field—but not by Manowitz.

It was his opinion that restyling could revive this neglected corner of the shoe industry. He gave moccasins color. He gave them white soles and laces. And once he began to see money come in, he did another revolutionary thing—promoted moccasins twelve months a year instead of just during the summertime. The dream of independence was accompanied by independent thinking. Manowitz's styling-promotion plans were as correct in concept as his revolutionary distribution idea. When moccasins were the Number-one shoe for the teen-ager, Huskies were making 35 per cent of the country's supply of them. "But," says Bill, "as we developed in the teen-age market and teen-age tastes changed, we were fast enough to get into the new items they wanted."

World War II and the years after added to Huskies sales. Women engaged in factory work discarded their high heels. After the war, women moved by the thousands to suburbs. Suburban living called for slacks, Bermuda shorts, a general increase in sportswear wardrobes. High heels were not only impractical with such clothes, they looked downright silly.

On the teen-age front, saddle shoes became a "must." What

is the popular style in your town? You may not know, but Bill Manowitz does. He learned early in the game that saddle-shoe-style preference varies from area to area. Stitching must match in one area, contrast in another. One section of the country wants prominent white eyelets in the lace holes, another wants hidden eyelets. White soles are popular in one place, all but tabu in a red-sole area. Teen-agers have to be "with it" down to the smallest detail.

Not only did Manowitz provide saddle shoes with correct details, he practically guaranteed total sales of the Huskies brand. First, there was his advisory service to jobbers and, through them, to retail dealers. Before a wholesaler placed his order, Hussco could tell him the sales potential of the shoe he wanted. Second, Hussco adhered to its prices and saw to it that retailers did the same.

Suppose aquamarine moccasions with white laces and soles suddenly "die" in Cincinnati. An order for aquamarine moccasins from Miami is filled by the Cincinnati distributor. It has cost Hussco money, but no Huskies distributor has lost his usual margin of profit. The money Huskies has spent to implement its exchange program is an investment in loyalty and good will. No manufacturer can step in and usurp the place of Huskies in its distribution network.

The exchange program is a large part of the reason why Huskies Stores have minimum markdowns. Another reason is that Huskies has established a subsidiary that will buy back "distress shoes" and sell them at a factory outlet store in Honesdale.

The entire production-through-retailer route is a neatly integrated cycle. Style (dictated at least in part by the consumer), quality, and comfort are built into the shoe. They are promoted on the national level. No retailer is more than three hundred miles from a wholesale distribution center, which translates into rapid delivery of wanted styles and eliminates the need for maintaining heavy inventories. No distributor is "stuck" with unsalable merchandise, for three reasons: Hussco will buy back; the company has predicted the styles it delivers on regional preference; and national advertising helps maintain sales "way up thar."

Bill Manowitz's concern for the independent retailer does not end with promoting Huskies to attract customers at the retail level. He has studied the problems of the independent versus the chain store and the mail-order house. His study has led to more than the unique distribution system that places no retailer more than three hundred miles from a source of supply; from it he has evolved a "markup-turnover" theory which he is always willing to expound.

"Markup alone," he says, "is definitely not the answer to the retailer's problem. There are many who think they are realizing their potential if they maintain their markup, but the problem is bigger than that.

"A retailer must realize something on his total investment, his entire inventory, if he's going to approximate his total potential.

"You have to figure your own total potential, because it's different with every store. But in every store it depends on turnover. Here's a very simple example of what I mean: Is it better to realize 50 per cent on your merchandise with two turns a year, or 40 per cent with four turns a year?

"If a retailer invests $10,000 in inventory, and turns it twice, he's grossed $10,000. If a man can invest $10,000 in inventory and turn it four times, he's grossed $16,000. He's put out the same amount of money—and sharply increased his profit!

"The reason the turn is higher with Huskies is because of the local in-stock service. The store does not have to tie up nearly so much capital in inventory, because the local Huskies warehouse is inventory!"

Bill's theory ties in with distribution, styling, brand-name promotion—three attributes of Huskies. (Theories such as that are often worked out to tie in with a situation as it exists. In reviewing Bill Manowitz's career, it is of important interest to note that the attributes of his wares and policies were formed to fit the theory.) Like the production-through-retailer route, the theory-through-practice story is a neatly organized cycle.

The sincerity of Bill Manowitz's beliefs is evident in the fact that he has eliminated price-cutting retailers. The years 1949 to 1950 were marked by a rash of price slashes. Huskies held their prices firm. Bill had his eye on the future; he knew what he was doing. The threatened recession was a bad dream that never materialized. Retailers gained new respect for the Honesdale champion of firm prices and fair markup.

On the wholesale level, Hussco's policy of protected sales areas is not just a phrase. A distributor who receives an order from a retailer outside his territory must forward it to the distributor covering that territory. He knows that if he were to forward it to Honesdale, the company would not honor it. Conversely, he knows that he is receiving the same protection. No one takes advantage of anyone else through Hussco.

On the other hand, Bill Manowitz told Quentin Reynolds, when interviewed for his appearance on "Operation Success," "I took advantage of big business when I was getting started."

Elaborating later on this remark, Bill said, "A lot of successful businessmen get a kick out of helping a young man who they think has something on the ball. They feel kind of frustrated if they don't have the opportunity now and then to do this. I've found that most people are afraid to sell themselves, or ask for this kind of help.

"When I wanted to get started, I was a mixture of brashness and insecurity, but I had enough of the former to convince the big suppliers of materials to the shoe industry that I could do the job I wanted to do."

What Bill isn't saying, of course, is that he took "advantage" of them by impressing them with his sincerity and ability.

Experience has helped other characteristics emerge; the magnetic one of leadership, for example, which has drawn to him a management group of capable young executives.

Bill considers business a profession, and, like other professionals, he is constantly studying it. Twice a year he goes to Harvard or Northwestern for a special seminar on business management at the graduate schools sponsored by the Young Presidents' Organization. He follows the business publications closely. "If business executives had to take a qualifying examination, as lawyers and accountants do, most of them would flunk it," he says.

Clear thinking and forceful, he nevertheless has an air of reticence and simplicity about him. A sophisticated man, Bill sometimes seems inarticulate to people just meeting him. It stems from a humility that won't let him use a three-syllable word if he can use a two-syllable one in its place. This can be fatally deceptive.

Bill works hard, and travels extensively. He has racked up nearly a million miles of air travel since 1938. And he is never without a camera. He collects cameras, both movie and still, and experiments painstakingly with them. He has a large library of movie film he himself took and edited. He also collects paintings, and has an excellent group of American moderns.

But all this might never have materialized, for the entire Hussco story could have ended in disaster and despondency in October 1942. Bill Manowitz had been in New York on business. Late at night, unaware that disaster had struck Honesdale during his absence, he drove into a service station about twenty-five miles from his home.

"Heard about the flood?" asked the attendant.

"No. What flood?" asked Bill.

"Honesdale. Hell of a flood. Wiped out the shoe factory."

Numbness and desperation were mixed in Manowitz as he pushed his car through the night, stamping the accelerator on the straightaway. His company was serving a rapidly expanding market. The year had seen great sales growth. The possibility of even greater growth lay ahead in the future—but what lay ahead of his headlights' reach?

He soon found the answer. A flash flood had crested quickly, roaring down on Honesdale with scant warning. It had torn through his factory, piling up silt, carrying away raw leather and finished shoes, tumbling machinery and piling silt upon it.

"The people were wonderful," he recalls. "They didn't have much warning of the flood, but they ran down to the factory. The men got together in gangs and carried machines out of the place. Other men and women grabbed up piles of shoes and saved what they could.

"Most of our Huskies were lost, and of course the men couldn't get all the machinery out. We weren't so big then as we are now. The loss amounted to $70,000. It was a lot of money. I could have been ruined, and of course a lot of people in Honesdale would have been out of work.

"But there are some pretty wonderful people in the world. I was able to raise $70,000 without any trouble from suppliers, and even from big customers. Almost before I could realize it, the factory was back at full production speed. We made up for lost inventory. We started to catch up with the expanding market, and before a year had passed we paid back every cent of the loan."

The "pretty wonderful people" knew what they were doing when they advanced the money to put Bill Manowitz back on his feet. A man who started with "a dream and a bankbook" worth $350 eight years before and had parlayed them into an Operation Success—you just can't wash out a man like that with a flash flood.

9. DANISH-STYLE ECONOMY

Svend Jorgensen of Wivel Restaurant

FOR A FEW DAYS DURING THE BITTER WINTER OF 1947 A Danish-born American stayed close to his bed. He was in a good London hotel, but good hotels suffered along with run-down hostels and office buildings and homes from the coal shortage. A bed piled high with blankets, bathrobe, and overcoat was the warmest place the tourist could find.

More than the crippling coal strike struck cold into the visitor's bones. He was returning to America from a brief visit to his mother's home in Denmark. The sight of poorly clad children and the absence of children's clothing in stores in that country was, to him, a chilling rebuke.

The visitor was a successful businessman in a highly competitive field, a restaurateur of international repute. He could thank his lucky stars that his wife and two daughters were not suffering from a fuel shortage. Instead, his mind dwelt on the plight of the Danish youngsters. Proud little Denmark was pulling itself up by its own bootstraps, rebuilding an economy crushed by the Nazis. What could he do about it?

The man who turned the problem over in his mind could have salved his conscience with a remembrance of his practical devotion to Denmark during the reign of the Germans. In a glittering ceremony, Povl Bang-Jensen, Denmark's chargé d'affaires, had pinned the medal of Liberation on the American Dane in the name of King Christian X "as an appreciation of your contribution to Denmark's cause during the years of Nazi occupation."

But to Svend Jorgensen, owner of New York's Wivel Restaurant on West Fifty-fourth Street, what he *had* done did not compensate for what he *could* do. The Wivel (pronounced Wee'-vil) had been "a home away from home" for visiting Scandinavians for decades. It had been an unofficial headquarters for Danes outside Denmark who were doing what they could in the fight against the Nazis during the Occupation. The intensity of war was past, but Jorgensen still saw a need among his countrymen, and he would do something about it.

The following year—1948—saw one of the greatest welcoming celebrations Copenhagen had ever given. Nationally famous figures doffed their dignity to carry signs welcoming "Uncle Svend." No wonder there was a celebration—"Uncle Svend" was returning with $40,000 worth of children's clothing. There were thousands of warm children in Denmark that winter who owed their comfort to the man who refused to rest on his past accomplishments.

In 1949 King Frederick IX knighted Jorgensen. Success and honor were well matched, for success had come to the Wivel almost immediately upon its opening and has stayed with it through the years.

The restaurant business is highly competitive. Add an orchestra and floor show, as Svend Jorgensen did, and the chances of survival diminish. Real-estate dealings and other causes force many New York City restaurants to change location, surprising native New Yorkers and bewildering infrequent visitors by the disappearance of landmarks. Many well-regarded eating places have difficulty providing service to their customers' liking. The quiet-spoken, silver-haired proprietor of the Wivel has avoided every trap.

Doors opened December 24, 1928. The Wivel has been doing business at the same stand ever since. One couple held a wedding party there and, a quarter-century later, celebrated their silver anniversary—sitting at the same table, served by the same waiter.

The quiet restaurateur left his native land in 1921, working as a waiter on a Red Star (later purchased by Cunard) liner. One of his present-day waiters, who has been at the Wivel since it opened, worked on the same ship. Both young immigrants had found jobs in a Scandinavian restaurant on Times Square when they reached the United States.

With typical Danish thrift, Jorgensen put away part of his weekly income. One day there was enough money to launch a restaurant. No one—not even Svend Jorgensen himself—can say exactly what it was in his character that made him strike out for himself. The opportunity of America? That's part of it. In the man, separate and distinct from beckoning opportunity and other outside influences, a decision grew from thoughtful consideration.

"I thought the American people would like a real smörgåsbord," recalls the former waiter who is the father of the smörgåsbord table in America. "Until I opened the Wivel, smörgåsbord was brought on a plate, just the way a waiter brings any other dish. Not like Denmark!

"I knew the Danish people in New York would like it, and I hoped the Americans would. Then I wondered about a name for my place. Oh, I thought of a lot of names, but I decided on Wivel, because that was the name of a famous restaurant in Copenhagen. Any Danes who came to New York would come right away to find out if my Wivel was as good."

Prime consideration was, and still is, serving good food. Strip away the *décor* and floor show, and the Wivel would still be a fine place to eat—and a place to eat well without rupturing family finances. Twenty-one of the Wivel's eighty-odd employees work in the kitchen. The masters in that area are the chefs who prepare meat, fowl, fish, salads, sauces, and delicacies for the smörgåsbord table. Danish pastry? Of course.

The emphasis on top-quality cuisine is unusual in night clubs. The determining factor is probably the proprietor's basic attitude or point of view toward his place. Is it a restaurant first? Is it a place of entertainment first? First and foremost, the Wivel is a restaurant. With that point established, it was obvious that portions must be generous; Scandinavians with small appetites are practically unknown. Further, a Danish restaurant shunned by Danes could hardly be expected to impress Americans as the genuine article.

The director of the Danish Information Office was feted at a Wivel dinner party attended by 210 guests on his seventy-fifth birthday. He, incidentally, founded the Danish Luncheon Club, which elected Svend Jorgensen its president early in 1957. The Danish ambassador, members of the Danish delegation to the United Nations, Danish seamen—including Captain Erikson of *Flying Enterprise* fame—all are Wivel customers. The late beloved Jean Hersholt was a frequent guest. Visiting Danish prime ministers, and Prince Oluf, during his American visit in 1948, have smacked their lips over the Old World smörgåsbord. Sonja Henie, Victor Borge, and Lauritz Melchior are among the well-known individuals to be seen enjoying themselves and their food at the Wivel.

Svend Jorgensen recalls a woman who had missed hearing Melchior at the Metropolitan Opera during her short visit to New York. It had been one of her prime objectives to hear the great tenor in person. Catching sight of him at the Wivel, she asked the restaurant owner if he would ask Mr. Melchior to please, *please* sing one song.

"Well, you know he couldn't do that. His contract would not permit it. He would get into all sorts of trouble with his manager and the Metropolitan.

"So," continues Jorgensen with a conspiratorial gleam in his eyes, "I had the orchestra play 'The Star-Spangled Banner.' Everybody stood up, of course, and nobody can say anything against a man for singing the national anthem!"

The Danish Symphony Orchestra held its farewell dinner at the Wivel before returning home. So did the Royal Danish ballet, following its widely acclaimed American tour in 1956.

It all adds up to undeniable endorsement of the restaurant by that segment of its clientele which is potentially its most critical.

The consideration of food might be called Departure Number One for a night club. Departure Number Two is the Wivel's entertainment. There is nothing in any act that would make the sternest parents hesitate in taking their children to see and hear.

The orchestra sounds a fanfare. Master of Ceremonies Bob Lee steps into the spotlight, welcomes the patrons, and turns over the floor to the first act, which is usually a young dancer. Next, a singer. Not a groaner, moaner, crooner, or vocal contortionist, but a performer with an actual singing voice. A magician or comedian may follow. Then Bob Lee returns to end the show with variations on a theme he has been performing nightly since 1936.

Prior to the floor show he circulates among the guests, asking a question or two of most of them. They are people from Pawling, Paducah, and Pensacola. Names are Danish, English, Irish, Italian. There are regular visitors and people on their first trip to New York. Two men are consummating a business deal, a couple is celebrating an anniversary, another guest is celebrating his first night "out" after an operation.

With the orchestra playing an accompaniment, M. C. Lee weaves names, home towns, and events into a fast patter song. It is a feat of memory and rhyming that astounds many customers year after year.

The first floor show is over in time for the theater-bound to be in their seats before the curtain rises. Most of the other guests remain to dance.

But even the most spectacular variety of acts fails to steal anything from the center of attraction that greets each arrival —the smörgåsbord. Svend Jorgensen imported the first refrigerated smörgåsbord table seen in America. The nearly overwhelming variety of delicacies it holds are carefully arranged in tiers, from the unadorned olives and celery to the glazed and decorated hams. Fish in many forms, sea food, pickles, a variety of salads, these are kept properly chilled on the table. Heated casseroles hold other palate-tempting treats—a dish heavy with mushroom sauce, incomparable Danish meat balls.

New York's restaurant-night club business is considered a sure way to grow an ulcer. Svend Jorgensen manages to take his time and enjoy his own food. He has not permitted himself to become hog-tied by a business which could do just that. He likes the work associated with running the restaurant, but delegates authority to responsible employees, which accounts for his never being tied in nervous knots.

Away from his place of business as well as in it, Svend enjoys himself. During the winter, he lives in Kew Gardens, on Long Island, with his charming wife, herself an accomplished cook, and beautiful blond daughter Vivian. His other attractive daughter, Doris, is married to a successful inventor and manufacturer. The family spends summers in a spacious, comfortable home on the edge of Lake Mahopac in Westchester County, forty-odd miles from the city. The tempo of midtown New York is left behind. The hospitable atmosphere is perhaps best described as "easy."

The same word can be used to describe the Wivel. Go back for as many helpings of smörgåsbord as you want. There is not the typical night-club annoyance of highly overpriced souvenirs being brought to your table. Even the hat-check girl makes you feel that you need not pay half the original cost of your overcoat when you redeem it. Filtering down from the proprietor's own manner, the air of ease is a reflection of efficiency and loyalty.

Svend Jorgensen's efficiency methods can be summed up in the word economy. Not economy on food and drink, but economy of himself. He thinks in a straight line and gets to the point, as is reflected in his economical use of words to express himself. While more histrionic persons wept and

shouted ineffectually about European countries overrun by the
Nazis, Jorgensen kept his own counsel and aided the Danish
underground. His is the economy that saves time to use it, not
to waste it.

Loyalty? You can see it in practice at the Wivel. Waiter
Andy is referred to as the new man. He's been there only
nineteen years!

10. GETTING THINGS DONE

Herbert Barchoff of Eastern Rolling Mills

"WHAT MUST SMALL BUSINESS DO? FIRST OF ALL, RECOGNIZE that it has no vested right in making a profit."

Who said that? A representative of big business? No. An agent of the government? No. A small businessman said it.

"Rather," he continued, "it must examine itself searchingly, and make sure that it is serving its economic function in our society. It must also decide whether or not its inability to compete profitably is caused solely by external conditions. Its poor-profit picture may be caused in part by bad internal management."

A cynical listener might have gathered that the speaker was an apologist for big business. A listener who knew anything about the speaker knew that he had stood up against big business, the federal government, and anything else that threatened the little businessman. "Bad internal management" had been one of his prime targets for years.

The Grace Line is a prime contractor in the government's fleet-replacement program. When it laid the keel of a new ship on January 15, 1957, Grace turned to the Small Business Administration to recommend a small businessman to speak at the ceremony. It was through the Small Business Administration that Herbert Barchoff was selected to be the speaker representing small business at Newport News, Virginia. That was the occasion of his calling upon fellow small businessmen to examine their internal structures. It was not the first time he had spoken in such a vein; it certainly will not be the last.

Barchoff is president of Eastern Rolling Mills in New York City's sprawling Bronx County. The county itself is complex. There are farms and tenements and apartments and mansions in the Bronx. There is one of the world's largest zoos and botanical gardens and old, twisting streets and modern traffic expressways. It is a pulsing, bustling community in its own right and the home of a million commuters who travel to Manhattan every day. The accent of its street urchins is generally considered one of the worst in the language; on the other side of the coin, the Bronx is "the borough of universities." Perhaps Herb Barchoff just drew on some of the complexity of his environment in developing his own many-sided interests.

Here is a brief word picture of the man today by one of his business associates: "Herbert Barchoff is one of a growing group of young business leaders who have successfully merged their business careers with active and intelligent participation in a wide variety of public affairs relating to the nation's economic and political life.

"With Barchoff, these range from the technical problems of his own industry to the broad new science of management, and from the specific problems of independent business to the economy of the country as a whole. It includes a deep interest in such things as the tariff question, good government, psychology, and education."

That covers a lot of territory. So does Herb Barchoff.

The fact that Eastern Rolling Mills was founded half a century ago by young Barchoff's father is of secondary importance in this story. At the age of eight young Herbert gave a piano recital at Carnegie Hall, which included a composition of his own. Magazine reviewers said he had a future on the concert stage. As a law student at New York University, Barchoff was brilliant. He won the Elliott Shepard scholarship and numerous public-speaking prizes, and was an editor of the student body's *Law Review*.

It is that outstanding record which makes Barchoff ownership of Eastern Rolling Mills of secondary importance. Endow a kid with talent, energy, and vision and he can be born in a barn or on a barge. In time he will find his niche as surely as water finds its own level. Herb Barchoff was blessed with those attributes—but being blessed with talents and using them are two different matters. Barchoff had them and used them—and still does.

Herb was serving as an aviation gunnery instructor in the Navy when the war ended, and Eastern Rolling Mills reconverted for peacetime industry. The fresh-out-of-uniform executive threw himself into the work of running the mill. He gained an awareness of the relationship and interdependence of government and business. Not an ivory-tower, "let's mull this over at luncheon" awareness, but a working knowledge of facts that he was to put to work time and again for the good of the industry and, incidentally, the country as a whole.

The first example of that type of action was a plan that young Barchoff drew up in 1942 and submitted to Washington. It outlined a method for channeling frozen inventories of copper into the war effort. The metal was vital. And it was hard to get. The metal had been frozen in the hands of manufacturers by government order.

A long-distance phone call from Washington was the signal for Barchoff to leave the Bronx mill for the capital. His letter had stirred up a demand for details. He drew up the basic plan for the Copper Recovery Corporation and became the youngest consultant in Washington. Copper-hungry America found additional tons of the vital metal pouring into its mills every day. The plan, its implementation, and the results it secured were largely responsible for Herb Barchoff's being appointed to the Industry Advisory Committee of the National Production Authority. He held that post until President Eisenhower dissolved the Authority.

It is easy to believe that Barchoff has "something on the ball." The country is full of people with ideas; not many of them hold a Navy rating one year, a Washington consultant job the next. The essential difference between the dreamer-type idea man and the president of Eastern Rolling Mills is his ability to *get things done*. As a one-time piano prodigy he knows that the finest music in the world is meaningless until it is played, and a plan is meaningless until it can be viewed in terms of implementation or accomplishment.

Barchoff's ability to get things done shows up both in his mill and the business world, particularly the "small business" world. Eastern Rolling Mills buys copper and brass from production mills and changes its specifications to meet the requirements of its customers. A manufacturer may require only a few hundred pounds of brass drawn to a specific thickness and slit to a given width. It is much too small an order for a production mill to handle. Eastern fills it. Several hundred orders may be required to consume the material Eastern buys in a single order from a copper company. To fill these orders requires a small mountain of paper work, a battery of precision machines, and a production flow system. Barchoff has updated the machinery and streamlined the company's systems and procedures.

Many small businessmen have looked at the advances of big business in the field of efficiency and turned green. "Big business can afford it!" is their cry. Barchoff found experts to do an efficiency engineering job for him on a contract basis. "I was told that I should know my own business," he recalls, "and the implication, of course, was that if I had common sense, I could figure out how to make the mill operate at top efficiency.

"That's not the way I saw it. You might just as well say that I should write my own advertising because I know what we have to offer our customers. I called in the efficiency experts because it was their business to know things that I don't. It paid off."

It paid off for others besides Eastern. By hiring outside experts to do the jobs for which they were trained, Herb

Barchoff was able to keep his sights up, able to keep an eye on the national business scene.

When the Korean War was gobbling up priority production, what he saw was calamity. Thousands of small businesses closed their doors. The epidemic of failures had to be stopped. Herb decided that he would try to stop it. The problem, as he saw it, was two-sided. On the one hand, small businessmen could not get raw materials to manufacture for civilian use. On the other hand, they did not know how to make the government aware of their production facilities. "The government itself," he says, "had only the most rudimentary setup through which contracts and subcontracts could be awarded to small plants."

It was 1951. Nearly ten years had passed since Herb had been called to Washington to put his copper reclamation plan into effect, but he still knew how to get things done. He called a "Shirt-sleeve Conference on How to Do Business with the Government." He sent invitations to thousands of small businessmen all over the country.

With that phase of the Shirt-sleeve Conference in high gear, he flew to Washington. Herb buttonholed Senator John Sparkman, head of the Senate Small Business Committee. He buttonholed General Lawton Collins of the Signal Corps. He tramped to the Procurement Departments of the Navy, Air Force, Ordnance, Corps of Engineers. He told them privately the same story he had proclaimed publicly—that if small-business plants were forced to close down, the nation would lose an important part of its defense potential.

At the eleventh hour confirmations were received from Senator Sparkman and seven other government representatives. Barchoff had been dealing with brass all his business life —but this was top brass. Generals, colonels, a Navy captain, the regional head of the Small Business Administration, civilian representatives of the Corps of Engineers—not a bad show to be staged by one man.

To house the Shirt-sleeve Conference, Barchoff erected a
huge tent in the lot adjacent to his mill. Hot dogs and beer
were served. A hot sun blazed on the big top, and it was truly
a "shirt-sleeve conference." More than a thousand small businessmen attended. They pelted the speakers with questions. It
was an eye opener for both businessmen and brass.

One outgrowth of the conference was a traveling exhibit
organized by the armed forces. It showed defense production
work which could be done by small plants. A second outgrowth was "United Action for Small Business," an organization that elected Herb Barchoff president. Shortly after its
formation, the group ran a full-page advertisement in the New
York *Times* which galvanized the government into action for
the benefit of small business. It called for certain legislation to
be enacted, the release of materials, and action by small businesses to protect themselves.

Just how many small businesses owe their present existence
to Barchoff's bold stroke is unknown. However, the epidemic
of failures was stemmed and Herb was on the road to prepare
for his next step. He had raised his sights from internal plant
affairs. He had taken action on the national level and was publicly recognized by being appointed to the Businessmen's
Group of the President's Council of Economic Advisers in
1952. Now he raised his sights to look across the Atlantic and
survey the business scene in the NATO countries.

The United States was pouring millions into the NATO
countries. One question bothered Barchoff: Was any of that
money going to European small business? You may ask why
he was concerned about six-man plants in Belgium, fifty-man
factories in France. Here is the nucleus of the answer in
Barchoff's own words:

"Recent history has shown that wherever an industry has
become a monopoly, that industry has been easy prey to nationalization. England alone has provided us with many examples of this. Unfortunately, British industry never recognized

the danger signs, clearest of which was the withering away of its own small business class, *the strongest safeguard in any system of free enterprise."*

Herb admits that he was an amateur when it came to traveling the European junket route. He went anyway, armed with a few European friendships, a few letters of introduction from the Mutual Security Agency, curiosity and concern about the welfare of small business across the Atlantic. His trip resulted in two articles in a leading business magazine—one on the subject "Small Business—America's Bulwark," the second propounding a graduated tariff system.

The first article warned the business community that a continual absorption of small business by big business would inevitably lead to monopoly, and that monopoly is the breeding ground of nationalization. The second article was a blueprint for levying import taxes on manufactured goods from foreign countries. In essence, the closer the European wage came to the American for the manufacture of a given item, the lower the tariff would be. This, Mr. Barchoff argued, would protect the living standards of the American workers and at the same time provide an incentive for improving living standards among European workers—thus gradually eliminating the inequities on which communism flourishes.

Again President Barchoff's action led to public recognition. He was one of three small businessmen to be appointed to the Capehart Committee—the Advisory Committee on Foreign Trade of the Senate Banking and Currency Committee.

Back in the midst of the national scene, Barchoff ran a three-day seminar on scientific management. It was called "Guideposts" and led to Eastern Rolling Mills sponsoring a free publication of the same name. The four-page *Guideposts* goes to metalworking plants and customers, combines trade news with articles on scientific management.

Barchoff has spoken at business meetings, conducted management courses, and made himself heard in the general press.

He hit front pages across the country by telling Associated Press correspondent Hal Boyle during the Korean conflict that small business was "being hurt more by a percentage war than by an all-out war."

He carried the battle before the Senate Banking and Currency Committee, arguing that big business was getting a disproportionately large lion's share of defense dollars. A few months later the newspapers quoted him as accusing the federal government of "headline defense planning." When 1954 threatened a recession, Barchoff made the business pages with his pledge of a "one-year moratorium on job layoffs" in his own plant.

The following year it was Herb Barchoff who took the wraps off the copper gray-market scandal. He pinpointed the gray market as the cause of copper prices being sky high.

There was a copper strike in 1955. The next year, floods knocked out 35 per cent of copper production. Barchoff, as president of the Copper and Brass Warehouse Association, was ready with a counterproposal to effect relief. He demanded an executive order to release 100,000 tons of stock-piled copper. It was the worst crisis in the industry's history. His open letter to President Eisenhower stirred up a furor. Arthur Fleming, head of the Office of Defense Administration, called him to Washington. The plane had hardly landed when Herb found himself in the midst of a battle royal with the Administration. He lost the war, but won a battle and a moral victory—the deferment of 11,000 tons of the precious stock-piled metal. The papers reported him describing it as "administering an aspirin when major surgery was needed."

The piano prodigy, the star law student, the aviation gunnery instructor, and the government consultant are names that you can give Barchoff at definite points in his career. He is a president, a traveler, a "management man," a fighter. One side of his complex make-up interlocks with the others; when the gloves are off and Barchoff is fighting, he knows what he is fighting about. Certainly he has never been harmed by the publicity he has attracted, but publicity has always been a by-product of his doing something else, not the goal in itself.

If there is a lesson to be learned from Barchoff's successful career it is this: Keep your sights up—relate different phases of your knowledge and experience to each other—when you know you're right, get in and fight.

11. KEEP BUSY ...

Charles E. Kohlhepp of Jersey Central Power and Light

"A BUSY MAN FINDS THE MOST TIME," ACCORDING TO AN OLD proverb. This, in part, explains the successful career of Charles E. Kohlhepp, president of Jersey Central Power and Light Company and New Jersey Power and Light Company, two important New Jersey utilities which, together, serve the electricity needs of 43 per cent of the Garden State.

Born in the city of Baltimore in 1896, Charles Kohlhepp at sixteen had to go to work because his father had died when he was fourteen and the Kohlhepp family needed financial assistance. He has been busy ever since. He looks back on the poor circumstances the Kohlhepps then found themselves in as "probably fortunate" for him because, he says, "It made me work hard both as to finances and education."

While still working he completed his secondary education at the Baltimore School of Commerce and Finance. Thirsting for more knowledge, he later added to his education by attending some night classes at Johns Hopkins University.

Looking around for a likely place where a young, ambitious man could test his mettle, he joined what is now the Baltimore Gas and Electric Company.

His career with this company was interrupted by the outbreak of World War I. Finding himself in the Army, through no choice of his own, he requested that he be assigned to the artillery, but found himself in the bakery shop instead, even though, with an eye to his military future, he had taught himself trigonometry and studied military and officers' manuals. Accidentally, he discovered that he had the second highest I. Q. in camp. Biding his time, he waited for an opportune moment and then told his story to some Field Artillery officers and at their suggestion confronted his superior officer with these facts, with the result that he was transferred immediately to the artillery. Within three weeks he was teaching some of his self-taught elementary trigonometry to some of his buddies.

In a way, this story illustrates one of Charles Kohlhepp's basic beliefs and one which he has followed throughout his business life. "Don't be 'licked' easily. If you can't get in one door, try another, but keep trying."

With hostilities over, Charles Kohlhepp turned his attentions to the job of shaping a career for himself. An opportunity developed at the Baltimore Drydock and Shipbuilding Company for a young man with Charles Kohlhepp's background and training. The company was owned by a group in Milwaukee. They also owned utility companies in Wisconsin and other states. It wasn't long before Kohlhepp outgrew his job as accountant with Baltimore Drydock and Shipbuilding Company and he was offered a job in Milwaukee. The Wisconsin Public Service Corporation was expanding and there was a need for bright young talent. Charles Kohlhepp was prepared to meet the challenge.

At the age of twenty-three he left Baltimore and moved westward, where he continued his utility career with Wisconsin Public Service Corporation, which today serves the gas, electricity, and transportation requirements of a large area in northeastern Wisconsin and the upper peninsula of Michigan.

For the next thirty-five years Charles Kohlhepp busied himself with this growing company. His belief that "a mind full of question marks helps self-development" proved true in his own case, and as the company advanced so did Charles Kohlhepp. He rose successively to auditor, treasurer, vice-president and treasurer, vice-president and general manager, and finally to the high post of president.

But even during this busy period of his business career he again found time to serve his country when, during World War II, he was selected for the important post of director of the Program Bureau and vice-chairman of the Requirements Committee of the War Production Board, a signal honor for a young man of forty-six. His help was sought again during the Korean War in the organization of the National Production Authority.

Charles Kohlhepp believes firmly in the principle that "good citizenship is a duty and not a privilege." He practices what he preaches.

While successfully guiding the destinies and progress of the Wisconsin Public Service Corporation he was identified with many civic activities as well as other business enterprises. He was a director of "Trees for Tomorrow" and the Wisconsin Valley Improvement Company, a director and vice-president of the "Greater Milwaukee Committee," a director of the Red Cross, and was active in organizing a committee interested in aiding Marquette University's long-range campus problems.

When the Milwaukee Expressway Commission needed a few members with proven, qualified background, Governor Kohler didn't have to look far. Among his choices was a man with a long record of achievement, Charles Kohlhepp.

At fifty-eight Charles Kohlhepp could look back with much satisfaction at a long and successful career, both in and out of business. He was in a position to take it easy, to "rest on his laurels." But Charles Kohlhepp is of different stock. He has an inbred love of work. In this respect, he says, "I was fortunate in my choice of antecedents."

Upon the retirement of the president of Jersey Central Power and Light Company, the board of directors looked about for the best possible man to lead this rapidly expanding New

Jersey company. Charles Kohlhepp was offered the job and
soon he was meeting new challenges. Returning to the East
Coast, he went to work on his new assignment with the same
vigor he displayed on his first job many years earlier.

Shortly afterward he was elected to the presidency of New
Jersey Power and Light Company, an affiliate of Jersey Central
Power and Light Company, and more challenges were hurled
at him. His job was to integrate the facilities and organizations
of the two companies—a Herculean task for anyone less experienced or with a less successful record of achievement and
administration.

Within a period of less than two years the job of combining
two companies was completed, and now, at the age of sixty,
Charles Kohlhepp is still busy providing the 325,000 customers
served by Jersey Central Power and Light Company and New
Jersey Power and Light Company with the best possible service at the lowest possible cost.

Charles Kohlhepp is rightfully proud of the record his companies and the electric industry have established in meeting the
tremendously increased demands for electricity while keeping
the cost to consumers below prewar levels.

What goes on in an electric utility company? We throw a
switch and electric power jumps to work. The jinni of Alad-
din's wonderful lamp was a slacker by comparison.

Many small utility companies sprang up shortly after Edison
invented the first practical electric light in 1879. There was a
wide scattering of such companies in the famed New Jersey
shore resort area. Later, when the demand for electric power
increased to a point demanding larger, more efficient installations, they consolidated. The consolidation became Jersey Central Power and Light.

The need for a strong president with an understanding of
the business becomes apparent when some of its ramifications
are known. What does go on in an electric utility company?
For one thing, it uses coal by the mountain. Jersey Central

feeds power through wire that would more than encircle the globe. Linemen are schooled and trained. Maintenance trucks are loaded from a supply inventory valued at more than two million dollars.

Electricity cannot be stored. It must be generated as required. The utility company has developed formulas to keep abreast of seasonal trends and requirements. Requirements are estimated even more closely by means of weather reports, knowing the outdoor temperature and natural sky illumination.

Men sit at control panels, watching the patterns of current flow from generating stations through substations (where high voltage is stepped down for our use) on illuminated wall diagrams. Let a breakdown occur at one point, and within seconds electricity has been routed in by alternate means.

To most of us the electric utility company is represented by the meter reader and the lineman. Behind them is an army of men, from stock-room clerks to engineers. We are all familiar with daring work performed by linemen in the face of flood and storm to maintain or restore power. Jersey Central showed that the same *esprit* exists "behind the scenes," too.

One of the company's tremendous generating stations is located in Perth Amboy. The quiet hum of its mammoth generators was overpowered on the night of May 19, 1950. Twelve hundred feet away, 450 tons of munitions exploded. In the surrounding area, thirty-three persons were killed, hundreds were injured, 3,000 homes were hit. Dangerous, unexploded land mines were strewn about. The power station was knocked out. Many of the men on duty were injured. Terror was in the air, yet the men stayed at their posts long enough to throw all the manual switches that brought in an emergency supply of current from other sources. Relief workers were not without the blessing of light.

When will disaster strike again? No one knows. Jersey Central Power and Light can contribute only one compensating factor—*esprit de corps*—morale so high that men will reject the natural impulse to flee for self-preservation. They will, instead, stay at their posts until they have completed their work. When the chips are down, such spirit is of greater importance than the wonders of the giant generators themselves or the great strides in technological advancement up to and including atomic-powered generating stations.

A man selected as president of such a company must have the ability to maintain morale as well as production.

Charles Kohlhepp points to the fact that, with only about 7 per cent of the world's population, the United States produces 41 per cent of the world's electricity, four times as much as Russia, the second-ranking nation, and attributes America's high standard of living to this vast electric power which makes mass production possible.

As a member of the New Jersey Atomic Energy Commission and Atomic Power Development Associates, Charles Kohlhepp is actively engaged in helping make atomic energy economical and feasible. He is busy helping speed the day when the atom will be put to work making electricity on a competitive basis with coal, gas, or oil, or even cheaper.

A strong advocate of a free competitive society and business enterprise, Charles Kohlhepp is constantly fighting against those forces which would lead the United States into statism or other socialistic ideologies such as have enslaved millions in other lands. He believes every American should speak out boldly and forcefully wherever and whenever this threat appears to encroach upon and imperil our cherished American way of life.

Charles Kohlhepp is an avid reader of good books, newspapers, and magazines. He keeps himself informed on local, national, and international events. He likes opera and sees every performance his busy schedule will permit. Baseball is his favorite sport; the Milwaukee Braves his favorite team.

If you ask Charles Kohlhepp as to what he attributes his success he will modestly reply, "being at the right place at the right time." If you push him for more details, he will tell you these things have helped him along the road to success:

> Keep busy.
> Keep learning.
> Keep persevering.
> Keep the "Golden Rule."

Already one of America's outstanding business and civic leaders, Charles Kohlhepp is still doing all of these things. He is still busy charting new courses—and new successes.

12. INGREDIENTS OF SUCCESS

Herbert L. Hutner of Mount Vernon Life Insurance

WHAT ARE THE INGREDIENTS OF SUCCESS? ASK A DOZEN MEN, and get a dozen answers. Always, however, there is an overlapping of answers. There *are* common denominators of success. The men who possess them are not all alike even though they share similar characteristics. They are tall, short, dark, light, serene, nervous, serious, lighthearted, talkative, taciturn.

Differences in personality are permissible, even in successful businessmen. One outstanding superficial difference is this: some possess the ability to isolate the ingredients that are responsible for their success, others can only "talk around it." Solid, smiling Herbert L. Hutner, president of New York's Mount Vernon Life Insurance Company and partner in the New York Stock Exchange firm of Osterman and Hutner, is one of the former.

Let's take the individual ingredients, then see what they add up to:

Hard work.

Diligent application to the task at hand.

Think deeply about a subject.

Keep abreast of new developments.

Be flexible.

Learn to take advantage of opportunities that present themselves.

Create your own opportunities.

Make an ever-widening group of contacts.

Enjoy your leisure.

Help others without thought of personal gain.

Add a dash of luck!

Hutner's list is just about all-embracing; at least it overlaps every known formula for success at one or more points. Of especial interest in this list, and typical of all, is the fact that the search for money, per se, is absent. No one underestimates it, but the point to be made is this: wealth is the by-product of success, not the goal in itself.

Russell Sage was a millionaire several times over but did not own a matching suit of clothes when he died. Hetty Green earned more money than any other woman in American business annals, yet she lived in a hovel. So the statement stands: wealth is the by-product, not the goal. Where it is the sole goal, it produces a freak rather than a success.

Environment played a strong part in shaping young Hutner's career. His father was a respected lawyer. It was natural that, upon graduating from Brooklyn's Erasmus Hall High School, the son would enter Columbia to study law.

"During my college and law-school days, I had my first jobs at a summer camp for boys. I started as a junior counselor, 'junior' meaning no pay. The summer I graduated from law school I was offered the job of head counselor at a salary of $600 for the season."

Young Hutner gave some deep thought to the matter and decided against taking the job. Instead, he became a clerk in a law firm—at less than $600 for the entire year. "Clients were scarce during the early thirties," he recalls, "and paying clients almost nonexistent. I was fortunate in being able to live at home.

"I was even more fortunate in being able to work with my father. He had been an active and respected member of the New York Bar for many years, although at that time he was more active in managing real-estate holdings than in practicing law.

"He was a great inspiration and a constant source of encouragement to me. He often told me that, granted average ability plus ambition, the key to success in a service profession was in making an ever-widening group of contacts. His theory proved correct."

Legal training has fitted thousands of men for careers in a variety of fields. It was to fit Hutner for his later career, and the shaping process began early. "In the field of corporate and real-estate law in which I found myself, the remuneration never equaled the time and effort I brought to the job. However, on occasions I would find myself called upon to give business rather than legal advice, and my aptitude in that direction often brought much greater rewards."

The young lawyer was spreading his wings. He was beginning to see that there was a world beyond his lawbooks. The fates started to work for him—apparently because he was already following certain pieces of established advice—following some parts of that advice was no hardship at all—widen your social contacts; enjoy your leisure.

Herb Hutner enjoyed tennis, his favorite leisure activity during his youth. He paid the not-so-nominal sum, in the early thirties, of fifty dollars to join a country club and spent as much spare time as he could on the tennis courts. One day Hutner found himself paired in a doubles match with Lester Osterman, Jr. "I didn't know anything about him except that he had a great forehand drive and we teamed up very well together.

"A few days later he asked me if I would handle the closing of a house he was buying. I was glad to do it, of course. Not long after that he called me and said that he had something on his mind he wanted to discuss with me.

"We got together for lunch. Lester Osterman told me that he had left Bond Stores—his father was one of the founders—then he said, 'Herb, I think you and I should go into business together.' I said, 'Well, how can we do that? You are a businessman and I am a lawyer.' His reply was, 'I don't think it

matters much what we do. I just have a feeling we could work
well together and that your legal background would be useful
in any field we might get into.'

"I told him that I would think it over and let him know.
With more than twenty years of hindsight it would be easy to
say that I should have jumped immediately at the chance. But
at that time there were a lot of pros and cons to be considered.
I gave the idea a great deal of serious thought. Then I got hold
of Les Osterman and told him I was ready to join him.

"In a fairly short time we had established an investment company. The second thing we established was our ability to get
along together as partners. We had our share of ups and downs,
and we managed to operate with some amount of success. A
little more than ten years ago we felt really sure of ourselves
and formed the brokerage firm of Osterman and Hutner, members of the New York Stock Exchange."

A decade of hard work and diligent application to the task
at hand preceded the formation of the stock brokerage house.
One by one, in pairs and in sets, Herb Hutner applied the rules
for success. At the time he was hardly aware of them as rules.
A job had to be done; it was done. Then another job, and another, until there was a long series of jobs well done, successful
accomplishments that indicated, as surely as a road sign, where
the successful future lay.

Once organized, the firm of Osterman and Hutner put all
its past experience to useful purpose. "Investigate, then invest,"
was its motto. The telephone became more than a means of
communication. It was the stethoscope picking up the heart-
beat of the nation's economic health and growth. In the course
of a single day Hutner would talk to the presidents of companies in Los Angeles, Houston, Toronto, Seattle, Atlanta, and
Chicago. The past experience of sticking to a hard job until it
was done gave him an ability to get at the minute, important
details required for making important investment decisions.

The "ever-widening group of contacts" continued, and still

continues, to be an important part of the picture. Often through these contacts the brokerage house learned of new developments or situations which offered interesting capital-gains opportunities in the securities field.

"Investigate, then invest." Whether a piece of news came firsthand, through the clicking Dow-Jones ticker or from a newspaper item, Osterman and Hutner investigated with a flair for economic sleuthing that may well make that firm name stand for the Holmes and Watson of the business world. "Whenever a change or event affected the holdings of our firm or our clients," says Hutner, "a personal visit would be made. We called on management to clarify our position in the matter. The trips were not always made at the most convenient times, and it might mean going anywhere in the world, but it was the sound way to know what we were doing!"

Herb Hutner felt that a stockbroker could learn much from actual participation in the business world. He became a director of several corporations, and activity on those boards gave new insight. "I've seen business in action at the policy-making level," he says. "It has given me greater understanding and has also helped me in analyzing corporate potentialities."

But even working at policy level did not finish Hutner's practical business education. In the early fifties his firm bought into Sleight and Hellmuth, Inc., a large manufacturer of printing inks. "It taught me a great deal," says Herb Hutner. "I saw the business at policy level and in operation as those policies were translated into everyday working practice. It helped me understand the problems of companies with which we came in contact in the securities field—problems in manufacturing, labor relations, cost control, personnel, marketing. You just can't afford to stop learning!"

Learning and growth are synonymous to Hutner. No one ever would have thought about *lack* of growth if his position in the firm of Osterman and Hutner had been the pinnacle of his business career, but between the inception of this book and the day it was ready to go to press Herb Hutner pushed on to a still higher peak. He and his partner turned over their Stock Exchange membership to Blair and Company, which absorbed Osterman and Hutner. Then they purchased the Mount Vernon Life Insurance Company and Hutner was elected president.

Osterman and Hutner is now a private operating company through whose facilities an interest can be maintained in a variety of companies. Sleight and Hellmuth remains an important part of the picture. Even more recent than his life-insurance-company presidency is Hutner's election as a director of Universal Products, Inc., a holding company with interests ranging from automatic railroad-ticket printing equipment to pari-mutuel machines.

Hutner operates from behind a large mahogany desk in a simply furnished office on lower Broadway, in the heart of New York's financial district. His manner is courteously brisk; it seems to say to the visitor, "Take all the time you need—but not a minute that you don't." Memos and messages for immediate and future attention stream across the desk without breaking the flow of conversation—calling for mental agility on a par with being a good doubles partner on the tennis court.

Quick efficiency is tactical. The man's over-all strategy is more deliberate. It is exemplified by the method with which Osterman and Hutner "takes over" a company. There is no "new broom" attitude. Rather, there is the realization that while new blood may be good, the old blood must be valuable, too, if it could operate the company at a profit. Hutner works toward solid growth of a company. You get the idea that if he used the phrase "fast buck" it would be with a sneer.

The ability to apply himself to the task at hand has led to a full life for Hutner and his family. Along with tennis, golf and water skiing are now favorite sports activities. He enjoys music, and so do his two children. They spend hours together exploring the wonderful world of music—and Hutner finds it no less relaxing because he can play only by ear in the key of C.

Other activities outside the office relate more directly to business. At the drop of an invitation, Hutner will speak about investing or insurance before an interested audience. Another person might consider it time lost. Not Hutner. His speaking has kept his finger on the gradually increasing interest being shown by women and by younger people in stock investments, and the business and economic world in general.

"Some years ago," he remembers, "I was invited to deliver a lecture on how to analyze securities for investment purposes before an economics class at Smith College. The questions those girls fired at me indicated a real interest in the subject, and I think it's a healthy sign.

"Chances are good that at some time in her life a woman will find it necessary or desirable to invest some money. All of the Stock Exchange firms are trying to assist in educating her." Certainly Osterman and Hutner did its share, and the same work is being carried on by Blair and Company.

The casual passer-by might consider a stock brokerage office an unlikely ground for growing a well-rounded life. The ceaseless interest in business and our economy, the books, periodicals, and up-to-the-minute reports dealing with those subjects. Phone calls, letters, and personal visits of clients—all dealing with business and the economic picture. But this, for the man who will make it so, is the heart of America; an exciting challenge to be met every business day of the year.

It was a challenge when the opportunity to gain control of Mount Vernon Life Insurance Company presented itself. Can a man, a partnership, switch from investments to insurance? Most of us view the two as being worlds apart; Hutner saw them as two sides of a single coin and saw the new challenge as more. There is the long-range potential of an insurance firm—something of value to hand down to a son, to a grandchild. There is the daily challenge of building solidly, of being at least partly responsible for a solvent pillar of our economy. Can there ever be a successful growth without emotional content?

The change to insurance called for more thought than Hutner had given Lester Osterman's original suggestion of a partnership at that memorable luncheon.

Herb Hutner takes the successive challenges in stride. After hours, or whenever time permits, there is more to life than the ticker and telephone, memos and messages. The business world is people, and for him there are the people who comprise his "ever-widening group of contacts." Mix activity with a happy family life, stir in the rules that Herb Hutner has laid down, and see what happens. As Lester Osterman remarked more than twenty years ago, "I don't think it matters much what we do...." Securities, stocks, pressed metals, printing inks, insurance, the blended ingredients add up to success.

13. OCCIDENTALLY ON PURPOSE

Max Hugel of Brother International

THE TELEPHONE BUZZED SHARPLY ON THE IMPORTER'S DESK. "Yes?" he asked through the intercom.

"Tokyo calling, collect," said his secretary from the outer office.

"Tokyo? I don't know anybody in Japan. Japan. Oh, put him on."

That is a reasonable facsimile of the reaction of four importers who accepted charges for collect calls from Japan early in 1953—calls that resulted in two of them ordering a total of 3,000 sewing machines.

The person who placed the transpacific calls (collect because he did not have the capital to finance them himself) is today the head of Brother International, Inc., America's third-ranking seller of sewing machines. The incident of the collect phone calls has been repeated thousands of times in salesmen's magazines and by word of mouth—but as the persuasive salesman himself will confirm, a few daring phone calls do not build a corporation, and a single incident does not make a president.

Max Hugel (he accents the second syllable) is a fighter in the business world with a reputation for fearlessness. As a battler, he is best likened to a scientific judo fighter who knows how to use the strength of his opponent to make him fall. Young—still in his early thirties—and energetic, Hugel gives promise of staying in the business ring for a long time to come.

The president of Brother International was born in Brooklyn

on May 23, 1925. His father died before he was born and his
mother found it necessary to work, so Max and his sister were
raised by their grandmother. An industrious streak in Max
became apparent at an early age. He sold newspapers, ran
errands, hawked ice cream at nearby Brighton Beach. These
"kid type" jobs may have played a part in shaping Max's future, but he gives more credit to his friends. "I was lucky
enough to make the right kind of friends," he recalls; "people
who knew things and who had nice homes." One of Max's
friends was a Nisei—an American of Japanese ancestry—and he
did play an important part in shaping young Hugel's future by
teaching him a few Japanese words and characters, although at
the time they were of no significance.

Hugel went on to premedical school at Brooklyn College. He
left to join the Army when he was eighteen. "A little while
later I was called in for an interview. They asked me if I understood Japanese and I said, 'A little.'" It was enough for the
new G.I. to be one of the 180 selected from 3,000 who were
interviewed to study Japanese at the University of Michigan.

Classes included Japanese history, geography, and culture as
well as the language itself. To graduate, students had to be
able to recognize several thousand characters. Hugel was one
of the hundred that graduated. He was shipped to Japan as a
second lieutenant and served on General MacArthur's staff.
The post gave him an opportunity to meet and talk with many
prominent Japanese, including the late George Murata, editor
of the Nippon *Times*.

Hugel began to understand and like the country, but when
his discharge came through early in 1947 he eagerly returned
to the United States. Stateside and out of uniform, he returned
to college under the G.I. Bill. His Army-sponsored studies and
the intervening years had proven to Max Hugel that the business world interested him more than the world of medicine. In
line with that change in his thinking he majored in economics.

Just how would the diversity in his background jell into a

business mold? Fate stepped in with a temporary but fast answer. Through a help-wanted advertisement, Hugel visited a New York importer who was looking for Japanese-speaking help for his Tokyo office. The interviewer had been Max's language instructor at the University of Michigan; he got the job.

Former teacher Roy Nakagawa, former pupil Max Hugel, and Bernard J. Etzin comprised the executive staff of the American importer's Japan office. Roy is a Japanese born in the United States, Bernard an American born in Japan. The three made a hard-hitting team.

"We gave that company a good year," Hugel remembers. "When Christmas came around, we expected to be rewarded with a fair-sized bonus. I came to the office all smiles. You can probably imagine how I felt—how we all felt—when the bonus turned out to be a fruitcake. Right then and there the three of us decided to go into business for ourselves, and we've been partners ever since. We organized the Asiatic Commerce Corporation with headquarters in New York.

"It was pretty rough for the first two years or so. For one thing, Berny Etzin was in a bad automobile accident and was out of the office for nearly a year. We imported toys, binoculars, small cameras, sewing machines, textiles. At one point the company operated the Flamingo Club in Tokyo. I was in New York at the time—never even got a free evening's entertainment out of that deal.

"Another time we manufactured several thousand vending machines, but we sold out because of the lack of time. There are only twenty-four hours in a day. For a while we made plumbing supplies, such as sink traps. Another thing we did was export toys.

"In Japan, as you may know, there are not many factories. The Brother Company has—well, I guess you can call it the foremost factory setup in Japan. Toys aren't made that way. People make them in their homes, and something we didn't know at the time was that many buyers go right into the homes and take the cream of the crop. People who just place orders but don't go into the homes to inspect get whatever is left. So our order for several thousand walking gorillas was changed into hopping rabbits."

On one of his trips to New York Hugel borrowed enough money to purchase thirty secondhand taxicabs and ship them to Japan. The cabs cost $100 each; shipping charges were five times that amount. However, automobiles of all types were in short supply in the Land of the Rising Sun, and it looked like a good proposition. The New York *Times* got wind of the transaction and sent a reporter to interview the enterprising Japanese-speaking Brooklynite. Probably it will never be known whether the reporter added two zeros in eagerness or to build up the unusual story, but the dean of American newspapers reported that Hugel and his partners planned to flood Japan with 3,000 secondhand taxis!

The Asiatic Commerce Corporation had forgotten to obtain an import license for the cabs, and the usually cooperative Japanese government found that a sufficient excuse to tie up the first wave of what was expected to be an inundation of old New York cabs. Three thousand secondhand American cars in postwar Japan could have been an economic disaster—and, after all, they had read it in the *Times*.

Finally a loophole was found in the law. The cars were auctioned. Max and his partners again bought the cabs, sold them, repaid the loan—and learned a lesson in licensing.

Days were busy to the point of being hectic. Max, Roy, and Bernie were keeping ahead of expenses, but they were not building anything. Toys, textiles, taxis, vending machines, a night club. It amounted to diversification with no reason beyond expediency. None of the original plans for the trio was being realized. They had done an outstanding job for their former employer; for themselves they were doing little more than keeping body and soul together.

It was a time for decision, and the decision was made in 1953. Max's bent for economics had led him into a study of Japanese products, against which he balanced a study of American needs. The dual survey brought him to the conclusion that the Japanese company they should represent in America was the Brother Sewing Machine Company.

Once the decision was made, Hugel and his partners did everything in their power to implement it. There was one large stumbling block. Nothing tangible—just the differences between the ways in which Americans and Japanese do business. The three partners visited Brother management, offering an entirely new concept to them—American representation and distribution, Americans doing the importing, Americans guiding the promotion and merchandising in their own way, to compete effectively for a share of the American sewing-machine market.

Audacity won the first fall when Hugel placed the collect phone calls to four American importers and proved to the Brother Company management that they could fill their quotas. Long formal talks and many cups of tea passed before Brother International, Inc., became a reality. By that time there was no doubt in anyone's mind of the sincerity of the Occidentals and their Nisei partner. They talked more than just dollars and cents. They talked markets, population, growth, and product improvements.

The partners celebrated the first amalgamation of an American company with a Japanese factory by dissolving their previous corporation. Now they were in Japanese sewing machines to sink or swim. In 1951, American sales of Brother sewing machines, which were not entirely unknown in this country when Brother International was incorporated, accounted for 10,000 units. Five years later, 652,000 were sold, making it the fastest-growing seller and third in rank among both American-made and imported machines.

Here is part of the growth story in Max Hugel's words: "We had very little experience in the distribution of sewing machines since we had only been connected with Brother as agents before this [the incorporation of Brother International]. Brother was very anxious to get its brand name over in the United States. At that time, of course, people who bought Japanese goods did not pay attention to the brand name.

"In 1954, Brother came out with an automatic zigzag. I was given the job of setting up national distribution in the United States—under the Brother brand name. I maintained the going price without too much trouble, but it was difficult to promote the Brother brand name. Nevertheless, I *had* to get Brother distributors.

"We offered a better profit margin than any other Japanese sewing-machine company offered in the United States—better than on European imports, too. Up to that time Japanese machines were being sold on the basis of any price that could be obtained. I felt that even if we sold only small quantities, we should start selling in the right manner. Our capitalization was limited, but we started to advertise in dealer magazines, and we began to pick up distributors here and there. We also started a little national advertising.

"Then we concentrated on extending our line. I made several trips between New York and Japan, each time to try to find another model—more streamlined, more advanced. In that connection I persuaded Brother to accept Mr. Sol Adler, a designer and inventor I had met socially, into the Japanese plant to help design new products; he is still in Japan. He helped design the Pacesetter model sewing machine in 1955."

But a lot more than that happened between the year Brother International sold 10,000 machines and its introduction of colored, two-tone, and fully automatic models.

There was, for instance, a nuisance suit instituted against the young company by a giant in the field. Not only did the sleepy giant make false complaint of infringement on a patent due to expire in six months, it also went so far as to threaten every sewing-machine dealer in the country with an individual lawsuit if he handled the Brother line. Dormant anti-Japanese sentiments were called into the battle. Distributors, including the oldest who favored the trouble-free Brother machines, were frankly scared.

The giant company had failed to reckon with Max Hugel as a fighter. The larger company lost both its preliminary injunction and preference for trial. Amazed dealers found they had a champion. Hugel's business judo brought a giant to the mat.

"Japan buys twice as much from us as she sells here," he says. "These sewing machines and other home appliances we are going to introduce can help her dollar balance. And if she doesn't sell to us, what's going to happen to Japan? She will have to swing into the orbit of Red China, or Russia. Right now she is our best bulwark against Communism in Asia, and it's only smart to do everything we can to keep her on our side."

Obviously Max Hugel's economic studies have raised his sights above the level of a sewing machine itself. He sees it as a product that can compete with American-made machines while it serves as a bond between the free Western world and Japan. One of his basic ideas, however, was a Japanese machine that would do more than merely compete. Toward that end he sired the design of the Brother Pacesetter, the most advanced home sewing machine on the market.

Step by step he visualized a machine that would nearly run by "thought control" as well as incorporate every advance in design that could be built into it. On Hugel's desk today is the "birth certificate" of the Pacesetter—his original ideas mimeographed in English and Japanese.

The plans were revealed and studied at a meeting of all department heads in the Tokyo plant. The new machine was to match America's taste for two-tone finishes. (Partially color blind, Hugel has unerringly picked popular shades for Brother machines.) The machine must have a "free arm" to permit easy handling of work. It must be *really* portable—weigh less than twenty pounds. The accessory table must pack into the carrying case, and the carrying case must resemble an overnight bag. The motor must be out of sight, in the arm. The work light must be positioned just so to give maximum visibility.

These and other points were discussed for days. The new model affected the entire factory, calling for a great amount of retooling. Brother Sewing Machine Company is one of the few Japanese factories that makes its own machine tools—the machines that produce the sewing machines. Workers in that department were busy for weeks making new tools, dies, and jigs. Colorists, engineers, researchers, and designers worked on their individual parts of the fantastic "thought control" sewing machine on which you merely set a dial to obtain the stitch you want to use.

When production models rolled into the United States, they made every other machine in a dealer's store look obsolete. So Max Hugel had hoped, and so he was told by more than one dealer and consumer.

In drawing up the "birth certificate," Hugel had gone over every machine on the market, noting what they had and what they lacked. As a result, he is happy to see Brother machines displayed alongside competitors' models. "We look even better by comparison," he says. Dealers who would once have paid a premium to secure Brother machines under private brand names now offered to pay a premium to buy them under the nationally advertised name. Brother had come of age—thanks to merchandising plans as well as design.

Hugel's research had acquainted him with a curious fact about sewing machines. There were many more in American homes than there were in use. Women bought them, used them, tired of them, and stored them away. That fate was good enough for competing machines, but the young president took a violent dislike to the idea of Brother machines being relegated to attics or closets. One of the greatest promotional assets a sewing machine can have is word-of-mouth recommendation— and women are not likely to recommend dust collectors lying in an attic.

The answer to that problem was another bit of Hugel business judo, this time directed at the retail customer. First, the new owner receives a complete home-study course. Whether she lives in town or fifty miles away, Brother sends the lessons directly to her at home. The course is an adaptation of the Bishop method taught in colleges. No pins or basting is required. Lessons are accompanied by patterns *in the customer's size;* when she has finished the course, she has a "basic" wardrobe.

After the home-study course is completed, the customer receives four or five mailings a year from the Brother Fabric Guild. The mailings make new patterns available, and through the guild she can buy her fabric at a discount. The Brother machine remains in use, the name Brother stays in her conversation.

An Ohio customer wrote the New York office to say that, much as she liked the home-study-course dress pattern, she could not use it. The neckline was low, and would reveal an ugly scar. Was there anything Brother could suggest? The letter was received in the morning. By nightfall an answer was posted, and with it a revised pattern for the neckline.

That is one example of Hugel's policy that all mail must be answered the day it is received. Only a few communications are of such a nature that they are held over. Air-mail inquiries get air-mail replies. Incoming wires or cables are answered through the same medium. "Delay an answer," says President Hugel, "and a customer can change his mind or talk to a competitor."

"It's a pretty rough policy at times," says Mrs. Ruth Ehrlich, who carries the twin titles of assistant to the president and advertising manager. "You know what mail can be on a Monday morning! But, do you know, Mr. Hugel's policy pays off. As soon as we receive a warranty bond from a new customer, we send a thank-you letter and ask the customer to let us know if we can help her. Some of them write back the most charming letters."

Reaching the Number-three spot in sewing-machine sales in a few short years is by no means the final goal for Brother International. "When you have a distribution setup like ours," says the president, "you can do anything.

"Take the Brother knitting machine. That will be our next big drive. There have been other knitting machines on the market, but none of them went over because nobody studied the market before.

"In five years, or ten, this will be a whole new industry in America, helping Americans and helping the Japanese. You can buy one of these machines for as little as $69. A couple of months ago we bought a knitted dress from one of the big department stores for $300 and duplicated it, stitch for stitch, for $11.40. That's what we'll sell—style, clothing, a whole wardrobe, and economy—not just a knitting machine.

"We are doing this a market at a time. As people learn what a knitting machine will do and accept it in one place, we move on to the next. It's five thousand times faster than hand knitting, and you can't tell the difference between what it does and hand knitting. Women will go for it when they know what it will do, and we're teaching them.

"We are doing more than teaching them. Each customer receives a home-study course, and when she completes it she has made a necktie for her husband, a sweater for the baby, clothing for herself. Then we start sending her new patterns and help her buy the wool she needs. Already our competitors have benefited from our advertising. We are making people knitting-machine-conscious, not just Brother-conscious.

"The knitting machine will raise knitting out of the socks and sweater category, and it will open up jobs for thousands."

One reason for the apparently slow market-by-market sales program is that it takes about two years to "put a machine over," as Max Hugel phrases it. "We have to sell the distributor. The distributor has to sell the dealer. The dealer sells the customer. Then he lives with that machine for two years until the guarantee expires. If he has trouble with the machine during that time, you lose a dealer. We don't lose Brother dealers. After two trouble-free years in a store, we're friends, and sales go up."

Other Brother products destined for the Hugel treatment include mixers, blenders, washing machines, washer-dryer combinations, steam irons, transistor radios, and motor bikes. The corporation president has ideas concerning each one.

At this writing he gives only thinking time to motor bikes. "They just haven't gone over here the way they have in Europe. One thing against them is that they're prohibited on parkways. Maybe a delivery model would go over. It seems possible here in New York." Who knows? Perhaps the colossus of our city traffic will fall to the judo treatment of a motor bike! If it does, Max Hugel will undoubtedly be in the winner's corner.

Planning and courage are evident in the man who has become president of Brother International and four other corporations. (His partners are officers in all five; Etzin is vice-president and Nakagawa secretary-treasurer of them. Recently Hugel said to Bernard Etzin, "I'm president of four corporations; you be president of this one." "No," replied Etzin, "I'm so accustomed to being vice-president I'd become confused; you be president.") Planning ability and courage he has, and obviously the faith of his partners. Here is what Hugel says about himself:

"There has been a great drive inside me because I have always felt a need, a want for security, perhaps because my early life was a struggle. I don't think that success has affected me in any way except that I feel satisfaction. I just can't stop." He paused for a moment, then continued. "It's not simply a matter of financial gain; it's a feeling of accomplishment that gives me the most drive—and there are so many things to do. I feel that there are still unlimited worlds to conquer in business."

14. IDEAS COME TO LIFE

John G. Berry of Kenilworth Steel

WHERE CAN A PERSON WITH AN IDEA—JUST AN IDEA—TURN FOR inspiration and guidance in this very material century of ours? There may very well be sermons in stones, but piling the stones into skyscrapers has not multiplied the value of the message. And the other traditional sources of guidance—the industrious ant and the bee, the river and Nature herself, are often hidden. The sermon in the stone is a needle in a haystack.

The person with an idea can turn to books or people, if he can find in one or the other pointers to the direction he is seeking. John G. Berry is such a person, a man of ideas to inspire men of ideas. He is the young president of The Kenilworth Steel Company, in Kenilworth, New Jersey, half an hour from the roaring heart of New York City.

Seeing Jack Berry today in his position with an expanding company, and learning that he had to climb the ladder from one of its lowest rungs, indicates that the man with an idea— just an idea—can make the grade in our competitive economy.

"Give me a good idea and capable men," says Jack Berry, "and I can't fail. That combination is worth more than money in the bank. Money in the bank can earn only a fraction of its own value. The right men and ideas working together can multiply earnings."

Many men in high positions have voiced the equivalent of that remark. Practically everyone pays lip service to ideas, ideals, and belief in people. In Berry's case the tribute to ideas and people does not end with the voicing of it. As is often said in the television version of "Operation Success," "Let's move in for a closer look—"

Kenilworth Steel is housed in a large building which is usually crammed with raw stock—coil steel from the mills—as well as machines that slit, shear, and reduce the thickness of the metal. In addition to the raw stock and the machines that form it to customers' specifications, the building periodically houses a nonprofit trade show, the Kenilworth Idea Klinic.

"I got to thinking," Jack Berry says, "that I was seeing a lot of good ideas in my visits to manufacturers and customers, and I heard about good, substantial ideas that my competitors had developed. Maybe a business could use half-a-dozen of them, but the men who should know about them would have to visit half-a-dozen trade shows or read about them in magazines. Everybody knows a businessman doesn't have time to read all the trade papers he should, and he can't visit every trade show he should. So I thought up the Idea Klinic.

"Look at the percentage of our economy that is based on ideas we hadn't even thought about a few years ago! Our economy *lives* on new ideas—ideas for processing, packaging, handling things. Maybe a company in Cleveland makes a new item that could save me $50,000 a year if I hitched it up to a new product made by a company in Bridgeport, but how would I know about the two things unless I just happened to visit the plants in Cleveland and Bridgeport?

"It seemed to me that that was leaving too many potential improvements to coincidence. Here, look at this." Mr. Berry opened a desk drawer and pulled out a money clip packaged in plastic. "One company had a new machine for embossing designs in metal, a second had a metal-shaping machine, and a third had an ingenious way of packaging in plastic at high speed. I got the three of them to team up. One stamped out the money clip, the second shaped it, and the third put it in a plastic bubble. These clips made nice souvenirs, and they demonstrated what each of the new machines would do.

"A lot of junior engineers and executives came to the Klinic the first day. The next day the chief engineers, the purchasing agents, presidents, all the high brass showed up. I got phone calls from Schenectady and Minneapolis. Would the show be on long enough for the people to get here and see the things they had been hearing about? And this, mind you, when it was a brand-new show that had run only a day or two.

"People *live* on ideas. You've got to. Labor wants things, but what is labor? It's people. People want things—more and better ways to live a fuller life. They're not going to get them, and we aren't going to prosper, unless we utilize new ideas to their full value. Living better doesn't depend on more money; it depends on the things that more money will buy. So, if you can cut breakage and spoilage, if you can make it possible for a man to produce more without increasing his work burden, you've added to real wealth.

"Companies that can't or won't meet the challenge are doomed. And there is no reason for not meeting the challenge, because there are good ideas waiting to be used in any field you turn to. And that gets me right back to the Kenilworth Idea Klinics again.

"We shifted our stock of steel around and made room wherever we could. We saved room by hitching up one exhibitor to another wherever possible. Our men kept right on working throughout the show, and some of our new processes were as much a part of the show as the regular exhibits.

"We didn't suffer. I know darned well that we picked up business as a result of the shows, but that was a bonus. That was beside the point. The real point—the way I see it—is that if business and industry stay alert to improvements—that's new ideas again—then our whole economy is going to improve. And if our entire economy improves, Kenilworth Steel is going to grow with it."

Those are realistic words from a successful businessman who has not lost his enthusiasm for ideas. If evidence is needed to prove that the Idea Klinics were started on an altruistic basis, it is to be found in the fact that Kenilworth competitors with new ideas and methods were invited to exhibit them right along with Kenilworth customers.

No, the piled-up stones that form the Kenilworth steel warehouse have no sermon carved upon them for easy reading, but in the offices and plant a sermon on success is preached every day. Boiled down to a few words, the message is this: Be alert to new ideas to improve your work and your service. Be alert to ways in which you can help your customers produce their goods better, faster, or at lower cost.

Do you think that the words lose their touch with reality because they come from a presidential peak? That they would have more significance to the mechanic or clerk nursing an untried idea if they were spoken from a lower echelon? That the man who talks about the value of sound ideas and capable people is buffered from the everyday world of troubles and trivia by his staff and position? The answer might be yes if Jack Berry had picked up the presidential reins from his father, or bought his way to the presidency by scooping up 51 per cent of the Kenilworth stock. But Jack Berry got to his job as president the hard way. He tested the validity of his ideas before he talked about them. Let's go back and see if we can discover how Berry got where and how he is.

His name appeared on a diploma from the Lower Merion High School, located on Philadelphia's Main Line, in the unpromising year of 1931. Jack wanted to go to college, but the condition of the national economy of that year was reflected in the Berry family fortunes, and Jack was forced to divert his energies to work rather than school.

He worked for a California electrical manufacturer for a year or so, then for a Philadelphia car dealer. Two years as a car salesman gave him enough money to enter the University of Pennsylvania's famous Wharton School of Commerce and Finance. Knowing how much effort had gone into earning every dollar he was spending for tuition, Berry cleared the four-year course in three years. That instance is typical of the driving force that has put the man in a position of prominence in the steel industry. Driving force, enthusiasm, interest in a wide variety of matters and people, a dynamic imagination coupled with a realization of the requirements to be met to change a plan into reality—these are characteristics of the man that you feel after knowing him only a short time, and the impression becomes deeper the longer you know him.

At graduation Jack was older than the majority of his fellow class members. He cites that fact as the reason he was interviewed by representatives of thirteen companies who visited the University of Pennsylvania that year. Whether attributing the number of job interviews to age alone is fact or modesty, Jack Berry was weighing the merits of the first twelve when he was interviewed by the thirteenth company, United States Steel.

It developed that there had been a mixup. Jack should not have been called for the interview. United States Steel was looking for accountants. Berry had no interest in the subject beyond avoiding it. In the relaxed frame of mind that came when he realized that he was not being interviewed for a job, Jack "let himself go." He talked about his selling experience, his thoughts on selling, his partly formed plans.

Just as in a storybook, it developed that one of the interviewing board from United States Steel was in the sales department. He was impressed. "I could never have talked the way I did if I'd thought that someone there was actually thinking of hiring me," Berry recalls.

The result, of course, was that Jack was hired by United States Steel and his formal education was augmented by that company's extensive training course. He saw steel made at the mills—ingots, railroad-car wheels, special alloys, bar stock, coils. In a relatively few years he was in the company's New York

office, heading up the Market Development Division. Then
came World War II.

Jack Berry slides over his year in the Army. "I got into
Ordnance and was wounded in the Battle of Aberdeen [refer-
ring to the Maryland proving grounds] so I was one of the
first to be discharged." Back in civilian clothes and wearing a
"ruptured duck," Berry could take his pick of many jobs.
Young, capable men exempt from military service were scarce;
America was their oyster. Jack could undoubtedly have carved
a whirlwind career for himself in a large steel company.

"I thought it over. It crossed my mind that the people who
worked for the large steel companies were driving six-cylinder
cars while the people in the small steel companies were driving
twelve-cylinder cars. Well, no, it wasn't quite like that. It
wasn't quite that simple to figure out. A lot of things had to be
considered. When I did make up my mind, it was to go to work
for a smaller steel company, a steel warehouse."

Warehousing, as it is understood in most other businesses,
is a small part of the operation. A warehouse in the steel business, however, is not a place that simply stores and ships steel.
Kenilworth Steel, for example, shapes, cuts, slits, and mills
coil steel to exact specifications for its customers. Newer operations make it possible for customers to obtain their steel with
textured or enameled surfaces. The customers of a steel warehouse require the metal in quantities too small or too fast for
a mill order, or their specifications include characteristics that
cannot be furnished by the manufacturing mill.

Kenilworth may have furnished the inside of your refrigera-
tor or small parts for your television set. The TV-set maker
may have required 20,000 small steel brackets, six for use in
each of his current models. The quantity sounds large, but
the total weight is small. A warehouse such as Kenilworth
takes a coil of steel, alloyed to meet the TV-set maker's specifications, slits and cuts it to length. If the steel must be reduced

in thickness, that, too, is done, and done within extremely close tolerances.

Jack Berry knew all that before he entered the Army, but he lacked the practical experience in the steel-warehouse field that would one day make it possible for him to become president of his own company. Not that he deliberately looked for a warehousing job as a step toward eventual presidency. He was looking for a job, in the field he knew, that would absorb his energy.

When he found the job, Jack went full steam ahead with characteristic force. Before long he was working in mills that specialized in different types of steel, while continuing to work for the steel warehouse. Jack Berry had devised and "sold" management his own on-the-job training program. This specialized, intense self-education, backed by his prewar experience with United States Steel, sent Berry back to the warehouse with great plans for developing stainless-steel business.

Developments and new business came thick and fast. Orders piled up. Machines hummed. The railroad siding, where the stainless raw stock rolled to the warehouse, was a constant bustle. Then it happened. Suddenly no one wanted stainless steel. The buyers of stainless steel seemed to have been swallowed by the earth. Anticipating an uninterrupted flow of orders, John Berry had had the warehouse purchase stainless steel ahead of production flow. The purchased steel continued to roll to the siding. Stainless steel mounted inside the warehouse and out. Some of the older heads around the warehouse wondered if the business would sink under the financial weight. Every inch of stainless-steel output, so it seemed, was leaning on their capital.

The doldrums lasted only five days, but they were probably the most fearful five days in Jack Berry's career. He learned a lesson about overpurchasing that he has never forgotten.

Jack's interests are many. He likes the theater. He likes music. He likes those two conflicting interests, golf and home life. To assure himself more of the latter, he put away his golf bag and turned his leisure-time energies toward the piano. "I'm not an artist," he says, "and never will be. But I can lose myself at the piano for hours at a time. Lessons cost me eighteen dollars an hour when I take them, but a psychiatrist would cost me a hundred dollars an hour, so I figure that I'm money ahead with the piano as an outlet." He is interested in other people's problems. He is interested in creative sales-promotion plans that will strengthen the country's economy. He likes both sailing and motorboat cruising. He is interested in business group activities. With all these, the one interest nearest his heart, except for his wife and four children, is his business—steel.

That interest is creative, not merely the interest that everyone has in the source of his bread and butter. For example, while Jack was with the steel warehouse, he devised a way to make cast rolls for textile machinery that is still paying him royalties and will probably continue to do so for the rest of his life. Instead of requiring stainless-steel plates, which had to be machined and finished in lengthy, costly processes, Jack devised a way to cast the outer shell of stainless steel, with a core of rigid, hard steel. The finished roller is perfectly bonded metallurgically, and the exterior is flawless. "It's part of my retirement policy," says inventor Berry.

One day at a casual luncheon with a man from Youngstown, Ohio, Jack talked about his pet subject—a steel warehouse of sufficient size, design, and flexibility to be able to service customers with a new degree of efficiency. Jack's vision of the ideal steel warehouse far outstripped his authority to introduce innovations where he was employed. His vision called for machinery geared to close tolerances and high production. It called for the type of flexibility that permits new installations when the sales department finds a need for them. It called for warehouse design and location that could be masterminded by the person who would do the principal job.

"See me sometime when you're in Youngstown," said Berry's luncheon companion.

It was a typical luncheon-table comment, expressing polite interest, not necessarily to be taken at face value. But Berry did have occasion to see Mr. C. M. Beeghly in Youngstown not too long after that luncheon. The subsequent meetings resulted in full capitalization of Kenilworth.

Business is booming for Jack Berry today. Sales continuously reach new peaks. "Show a man how he can increase production or efficiency or cut down waste, and you don't even have to ask him for an order," says the steel man, briefly summing up the creative approach to selling by serving an existing need.

The person with an idea—just an idea—may not find a sermon carved on the building stones of Kenilworth Steel, but the message is there. Look at the building if you are in the vicinity. The building is only an idea—an idea come to life, sprung from the mind of Jack Berry. Perhaps *your* idea, *your* vision is on tomorrow's drafting table.

15. THE FATHER OF WEAPONS' CONTROL

Hannibal Choate Ford of Ford Instrument (and his successor, Raymond F. Jahn)

THE DAWN CAME SLOWLY—SLOWER, IT SEEMED, AS THE "COUNT down" neared zero. The intense men in the control center kept a tense vigil over their sensitive recording instruments. Suddenly the sky was green, blue, and purple. The dim early light of morning revealed a monolith of steel on the field beyond the control center. A crisp, metallic voice blared over the public-address system: "T—seconds . . . —4 . . . —3 . . . —2 . . . —1 . . . zero—MARK!" A roar! A burst of red-orange flame. Then it happened. The monolith began to rise. Slowly at first, then with incredible speed it leaped skyward toward its target.

In seconds it was high in the sky, a silver javelin tossed by science. But, unlike a javelin, the hurtling steel shaft had a sense of direction, a "brain" that acted as pilot and navigator, guiding the flame-spouting tube of destruction toward its target. As surely as the needle of a compass is drawn to the mother lode—as if by magic the javelin of science found its mark, exploded, and destroyed the target.

Firing a missile is a delicate operation. Guiding a missile in flight is an engineering miracle that cannot depend on magic. To make a missile *think* takes scientific know-how; to create machines that solve complex mathematical problems instantaneously takes vision. To turn this know-how, this vision, into a reality takes highly skilled men and women. It takes an organization that can look toward the future and develop in the present. Those who realize these facts point to Ford Instrument Company of Long Island City, New York, as one of the finest examples of this type of industrial development.

Many men and women are part of the company, but the organization is best exemplified by its leaders, past and present. Hannibal Choate Ford was the founder of the company that bears his name. Hannibal—who was no relation to Henry Ford —succeeded in building, not just a company, but a new industry for himself and the country.

You never heard of him? If you haven't, it is not surprising. Because of the nature of his work, Ford gained almost complete anonymity. He was often referred to as "the United States Navy's best-kept secret since World War I" when the application of his genius had its first "pay-off." By those intangible standards that measure the greatness of original thinkers, Hannibal Choate Ford easily takes his place at the zenith with an Edison or a Marconi.

Ford gained this tribute from Vannevar Bush, the man who directed the nation's scientific research during World War II: "There were two things which revolutionized warfare—automatic gunfire computers and the internal-combustion engine."

Ford developed the first automatic gunfire computer, but before this monumental development could take place he had to gain the knowledge and experience required to transform an abstract idea into a reality. Perhaps it all started in the office and shop of the Dryden (New York) *Herald,* the small-town weekly that Millard Ford, his father, owned and published. You can imagine the small boy, with his mechanical bent and imagination, watching with fascination the rhythmic action of the old-style printing press: the inked rollers moving back and forth over the type, the long, thin arm that fed the paper into the press, and the turning of the big black wheel. It must have been nothing short of magic for him to see a sheet of blank paper one moment, and the next to see it covered with black marks. And the magic stayed with him. Many years later, when Ford was at the head of his own company, he still found time to tinker with a friend's printing press.

Ford was as close to being a natural mechanic as any man could be. When he was only eighteen he was employed in the experimental department of the Daugherty Typewriter Company in Kittanning, Pennsylvania. A year later he was a tool-maker for the Westinghouse Electric and Manufacturing Company. It was good practical experience, but Ford had a burning desire to learn and to know—to know all about physics, mathematics, and mechanics, which would be the harness to control his dreams. In 1899 he entered Cornell University. Four years later, at the age of twenty-six, he graduated with a degree in electrical engineering. His schooling was not all in the realm of theory; while at Cornell, he obtained spare-time employment in the University's Electrical Engineering Laboratory to help finance his learning. In the lab he took his initial step in applied science. He built the first cathode-ray oscillograph to be used in this country for wave form and power determination—the instrument which was to become the stethoscope of engineers in our electronics age.

In 1953, fifty years after its founder had graduated from Cornell, the Ford Instrument Company established the Hannibal C. Ford fellowship. It provides funds for a year's study at the Graduate School of Cornell University.

In 1906 Ford was granted a patent for a system that controlled the speed of trains where traffic is congested, as in the New York City subway system. The basic ideas for this invention are still in use. Other early patents covered improvements of typewriters and business machines. By 1909 Ford had become Elmer A. Sperry's chief engineer, when the Sperry Gyroscope Company was organized. In that capacity he assisted in the development of the gyrocompass. The gyrocompass can hold a ship on a given course better than a human can do the job. Later, when aircraft adapted the invention, it became the nucleus of the automatic pilot.

In 1915 Ford struck out on his own. He convinced a group of businessmen to back him in the formation of the Ford Marine Appliance Corporation, a feat indicating the realistic businessman as well as the farsighted visionary. The purpose of the corporation was to explore and develop fire-control equipment for the Navy. Up to that time the aiming and firing of naval guns were controlled by a group of mathematicians in uniform who sat around a table aboard ship solving problems in trigonometry. Their answers gave the gunners the direction and angle of elevation at which to fire. But by the time a problem was solved, the target was usually out of range. Ford sold his backers the idea of a machine that would instantaneously solve the problems, and so the corporation was launched. A year later it was reorganized as the Ford Instrument Company. In 1930 Ford became its president. He was active in the company until 1943. In 1915 it had about fifty employees; during World War II its staff had grown to 8,000 —a certain indication of the importance of the new industry Ford had fathered.

Like so many other gifted greats in the fields of science and business, Ford turned to music for relaxation. His instrument was the flute, and while at college he was a member of the symphony orchestra. But even above music he rated as his greatest joy just plain tinkering. He was a "do it yourself" specialist long years before anyone used that phrase. Some of the old-timers at Ford Instrument will tell you, "Sure, I knew him. He'd come around looking for discarded gears or anything else that somehow he could find a use for." His motto was, "I would construct a machine to do any old thing in any old way"—a motto more indicative of attitude than method— and so, invariably, he would find a use for the old gears and "junk."

A typical example of his ingenuity and an insight into his

sense of humor stood outside his home at Kings Point, Long Island. Ford acquired a giant bronze eagle, a former ship figurehead. He mounted the bird atop a high stone pillar on a revolving table which permitted it to be turned automatically toward an approaching boat. To complete the hoax of the observant eagle, he wired it so that authentic eagle screams came from the bronze bird at the touch of a button. Many a Long Island Magellan was amazed—if not frightened half to death—by the "watchdog" eagle.

Although Ford knew he was creating a new industry that someday would be a giant, he never lost sight of the people who worked for him. He was genuinely fond of them, even when they left his employ to strike out on their own. He admired initiative in any man. Ford tried to make his company a new kind of family, an industrial family, a place into which a father might bring his son with pride. The Ford Instrument Company of today boasts of entire families working together. Typical of Ford's attitude was the yearly weekend party held at his home for employees. Everyone attended, including the children. But it was not so much the yearly party that endeared him to the men and women who knew and worked for him. It was the little details. Ford remembered their names, when this one or that one was married, the names of their children, their birthdays. Ford never forgot that they were *people*, and they remember him vividly.

Stories are still told about the sketches he drew for new equipment—how he went over the original lines with a soft, blunt pencil so that the final drawing was a big black blob. But later, when the sketch was deciphered, it represented a piece of original machinery. Ford's tireless energy astounded those who worked for him. Only after he finished a project did he realize that perhaps he had not slept for two or three nights, or that he had not eaten a meal in as long a period of time.

But there is more to be remembered than the characteristics

which endeared him to those who knew him. Ford was an intrepid explorer in the field of applied science. He had the amazing talent of being able to utilize abstract mathematical and physical laws, to develop machines that "think." He accomplished this by working out intricately arranged systems of gears, by designing special cams that represent trigonometric functions, differentials that will add or subtract, and mechanical integrators able to solve problems of distance and time down to split seconds. With these Ford produced a successful machine which instantaneously solved fire-control problems from the deck of a ship. The ship itself is moving. Its target is moving. The distance between them is changing. Their direction in relationship to each other is changing. Wind speed and direction affect the problem. Ford's machine absorbed every factor, gave an immediate answer; he was truly the father of fire control.

The device was known as Range Keeper Mark I and was installed on the U.S.S. *Texas* in 1917. Approximately ten years later Ford produced a director that solved the far-more-complex problem of antiaircraft fire control from the deck of a moving ship. The device had a total of 55,000 moving parts! Admiral Oscar C. Badger, USN (Ret.), said of the director, "It put our Navy technically ahead of any other in the world. In my opinion, it was one of the most remarkable pieces of machine design in modern times."

Hannibal Choate Ford left his mark in the world. When he died on March 12, 1955, we lost one of our greatest applied scientists, one of the last of the pioneers who gave us technical "know-how" in a manner and of a quality to guide those who followed.

Today the man who holds the helm at Ford Instrument Company is Raymond F. Jahn, who knew and worked in close association with Ford for many years.

Ray Jahn was born in the late summer of 1900, when twenty-three-year-old Hannibal Ford was already laying the groundwork for his future career. Jahn's father, Frederick G. Jahn, was the inventor of the automatic stamp-canceling machine used by the post office. As a young man, Raymond showed an early predilection to follow his father's footsteps.

He graduated from Manual Training High School in Brooklyn, New York, at the age of nineteen, following an interruption in his senior year, when he decided to join the Army Air Force. The day he reported for duty at Mitchel Field was November 11, 1918. The war was over. The young "eagle" was honorably discharged six weeks after he had taken the oath. Back to high school he went. In order to finish with his class, he had a lot of work and lost time to make up. He did it by convincing the school authorities that he should be allowed to take a double program, and he managed to attain grades that permitted him to go on to college.

It was at this point that Jahn began following, although unknowingly, in Ford's footsteps. He attended Cornell University, where he received his degree in mechanical engineering. Two years later he married the former Helen E. Rogers. They have two children, Raymond, Jr., and a daughter, Jeryl. By way of coincidence, Raymond, Jr., was sworn into the Navy on the day World War II ended.

Jahn became a machine designer for the American Pencil Company when he graduated from college. A year later he joined the staff of the International Postal Supply Company, the company for which he had worked during his Cornell vacations. In 1927 he joined the Ford Instrument Company while waiting for a patent to be awarded on a check-canceling machine. For him it was to have been a temporary position. But three decades have passed and he has attained a position that many men dream of but few are capable of reaching. "It was chance," he says. "I happened to be in the right place at the right time." But chance has a way of being on the side of the person who has prepared himself for a higher position.

At fifty-six, President Raymond Jahn still retains the lean-

ness of youth. He is a tall man. His features are sharp, even
to the long lines that arc down from his nostrils to the corners
of his mouth. He speaks softly and with complete frankness.
He possesses a quiet sense of humor; when something amuses
him, a smile slips across his face and sparkles in his eye.

Apart from being an executive, from carrying the burden
of countless decisions, Ray Jahn occupies himself with outside
interests. A devoted baseball fan, he also recalls the days when
he played hockey for Manual Training High and later at
Cornell. But, having followed H. C. Ford through college and
into the presidency of his company, he has again followed the
father of fire control in outside interests. "I'm a 'do-it-your-
self, all-around fix-it man,' " he says, and by way of illustration
can point to his summer home, which he completely renovated
with the barest minimum of outside help. Because it gives him
a tremendous feeling of creativeness, he enjoys working with
wood more than with any other material.

Indeed, Raymond Jahn resembles his predecessor in many
ways. Although success has touched him, he attributes it to
chance and has never lost sight of the fact that many people
have not been half so lucky. And the two men seem to have
been graced with that special ingredient all men of accomplishment possess. In their case, if it concerned machinery,
nothing was impossible. They seemed to differ only in their
ages. When Jahn joined the company, Ford was already fifty
years old, had already established for himself an incredible
record of engineering achievement. The previous year he had
perfected the antiaircraft gun director with its 55,000 moving
parts.

Today, under Jahn's guidance, Ford Instrument Company
still retains much of the relationship between employer and
employee established by Ford. Raymond Jahn himself has
helped this by establishing at Ford the first industrial cancer-
detection clinic, a program that has saved the life of more
than one employee.

Jahn realized the need for such a clinic when the dread hand of cancer struck in his own family. He knew that if the malady had been recognized in time, the untimely death would have been averted. So that members of the Ford industrial family might be spared that tragic realization, he spent untiring effort on the project. With the assistance of the company's consulting physician, the clinic was established. After hours he is active on the Queens County Cancer Committee.

Although many of the products that Ford Instrument Company develops and manufactures are for the armed forces, Jahn takes pride in the company's efforts to beat its electronic swords, as it were, into electronic plowshares. One Ford development, for example, is a navigational device for the Air Force that tells the pilot of a plane exactly where he is above the earth, where he is in relation to his point of departure, how far he has to travel to reach his destination. A device such as this would be of inestimable value to civilian aircraft. The heart of the instrument is a cam, an odd-shaped piece of metal resembling a potato more than Hollywood's versions of aircraft guidance devices. If you saw one lying in the street—highly improbable—you would take it for a piece of scrap metal.

Another field which the company is exploring is that of atomic power for civilian and marine use. This is an outgrowth of the company's work on the controls for the atomic submarine *Seawolf*.

In talent, in interests, in abilities, and hobbies, in his belief that *"It can be done,"* and in his feeling for those who work for his company, Raymond Jahn seems to be a later edition of the original work which was titled Hannibal Choate Ford.

16. TAKE A GIANT STEP

Henry Peterson of Feature Ring

FINGER RINGS HAVE BEEN IN EXISTENCE SINCE THE DAYS OF THE ancient Egyptians and Babylonians—perhaps longer. Just about every metal and method of adornment known to mankind have been used to adorn fingers. Quite literally, there have been millions of styles of rings. It would seem that in the course of a few thousand years every possible style and innovation would have been exhausted. But Henry Peterson proved that there were untried styles and innovations in the designing, making, and marketing of rings—and proved it the hard way, starting with the shape of a ring: zero.

Peterson was born in London. His father died when he was very young. His mother, a woman of courage and determination, brought her children to the United States. She had lived here before her marriage and wanted her children to be brought up as Americans.

Henry was born in 1908—probably a year that no one would have chosen if he could have foreseen the general economic ups and downs that lay ahead for the business world. Persons born then were too young to take advantage of the skyrocketing business world of the middle twenties and just old enough to be looked upon as a means of support when the business world had few opportunities to offer.

Even during his abbreviated schooling, young Peterson worked for the family. He delivered baked goods before school and worked in a candy store afternoons and evenings. During the summer he sold soft drinks. At the age of fourteen the family's low finances forced him to quit school, get his working papers, and go to work in earnest. His dream of educating himself to become an electrical engineer was short-lived.

With some difficulty he found a job as an apprentice jewelry engraver on New York City's Canal Street. His starting pay—zero. That was his salary for several weeks as he learned how to handle the tools of the craft. His first actual pay was three dollars a week. Later it mounted to five and subsequently it doubled. One day a spirited argument with the shop foreman led to Peterson quitting his job.

He found a second job farther uptown in New York City and stayed there several years. When the firm merged with a manufacturing concern, it did not take long before his talents were recognized and he was made supervisor of the Engraving Department. As supervisor, he had access to all rings at the time of final finishing. It was then that he began to develop ideas and create new methods which would improve the rings' over-all appearance. Then came the depression—and the company, as did many others in the luxury field of jewelry, folded up, leaving young Peterson high and dry.

"Naturally," he recalls, "I went to other manufacturers to see if they had anything. Wherever I went it was the same story—no jobs anywhere because there was no business."

Now watch determination go to work.

"Out of sheer necessity I had to do something, and as there were no jobs available, I decided to go into business for myself. I approached a diamond setter who was a friend of mine. I told him that I was out of work and wanted to rent bench space from him. Of course I had to tell him I had no money to give him, but I asked how much rent he would want if he did agree to let me have the space, and he said, 'Ten dollars a month.' "

The desire, the will to do something despite the condition of the economy in general and the condition of the jewelry business in particular, must have struck the diamond setter. He invited young Peterson to start using the bench space and to pay him when he had the money.

"I started to work there with one bench. It was just about as wide as a window. I went from one building to another, knocking on every door where I thought they could give me some engraving work. Oh, I got some work, but hardly enough to eat on.

"At the end of the month I wasn't in a position to pay my ten dollars' rent. My friend told me not to worry about it. Times would get better. So I hung on for several months. I had paid him ten or fifteen dollars and still owed him ten or fifteen when something really disheartening occurred. Some of the people he did work for objected to my being in his place. They said I might be copying some of their designs. So, of course, my friend, in order to protect his own business, even though he knew that their suspicions were groundless, had no choice but to ask me to leave.

"When I left that space, I contacted a watch-band manufacturer. He was willing to partition off about the length of two windows in his place and let me have the space for twenty dollars a month. What was I to do? If I couldn't afford ten, how was I to afford twenty?

"My sister loaned me twenty-five dollars. I paid the watch-band manufacturer his first month's rent, rented out half my space to a diamond setter—and was right back to my ten dollars a month."

Today Henry Peterson is president of Feature Ring Company, the world's largest manufacturer of wedding and engagement rings. He will give out no sales figures, but the extent of his business may be gauged by the fact that he pays more than $45,000 a year in rent for his mid-Manhattan factory and office space. His personal income is in six figures. But he clearly remembers the depression days when nickels and dimes had to be fought for.

For a few months his subletting arrangement worked out,

but only because he, in turn, was subletting half of his small space. Then the watch-band manufacturer, tired of acting as an in-between rent collector, turned over the partitioned space to the landlord. A month or two later the diamond setter had to surrender his bench space. He was unable to meet his half of the rent. Young Peterson dug in desperately for a toehold on the cold, bleak face of the nation's economy.

One day Henry Peterson sat alone in his two-by-four shop. His only visitor that morning was the landlord. "He dispossessed me. I went down to see another tenant, a man who sent me whatever engraving work he had. I told him that I could no longer work for him, that I had been dispossessed because I didn't have twenty dollars.

"Fortunately, he liked the quality of my work and the speed with which I delivered it. He wanted me to continue in business so he loaned me twenty dollars. Several days later I met the agent in court and paid him the rent, whereupon he agreed to drop the dispossess proceedings. I then said to him, 'Someday you won't have a place big enough for me.' "

It may have been sheer bluff that led Henry Peterson to make so bold a statement. Later events proved him right, but the agent must have wagged his head many times over the aggressive youngster's unbelievable statement. No real-estate agent would believe such a prophecy in the middle of the depression.

"I started to do better. Things started to happen. More work came in. I could make twenty-five dollars a week by working until two o'clock every morning. For a year or more I worked that way, Saturdays and Sundays included. I had to be my own errand boy, making pickups and deliveries as well as answering the telephone and taking care of office details, so of course I had to put in extra hours."

Then came Peterson's first big break. A large ring-manufacturing plant in New Jersey was having production difficulties. The plant supervisor knew Peterson to be a hard-working,

talented young man. He asked Peterson if he would be willing
to set up an assembly operation on a contracting basis. Peterson
was overjoyed but bewildered. Here was his opportunity to
take his first giant step.

"The only way I could do it," he recalls, "was to get hold
of a jeweler I knew who was working on a WPA job. He was
a bit skeptical, of course. 'How long will the work last?' he
wanted to know, and of course I could not tell him. However,
he agreed to work with me and do the assembly work. That
and the engraving work I was able to pick up on the outside
kept me pretty busy for a while."

Pretty busy! Peterson, not yet thirty, had put in more working hours than most men of fifty. Nor was he, even then,
finished with cramming two to two-and-a-half working days
into twenty-four hours.

"One day in 1935 I had a caller from one of the country's
largest jewelry jobbing houses. Some of the work we had done
for the Jersey firm had gone to them. The caller asked if I
would do some assembly work for them on parts bought in the
New York area.

"When he asked me that, I almost sank through the floor.
My visitor wanted me to do complete assembly jobs and engraving for what I considered to be the biggest jobber in the
whole United States. I was flabbergasted. It was too good to
be true. But—I didn't even know how much to charge. I didn't
know how to quote a price on a complete job."

Whether Henry Peterson realized it or not at the time, this
was to be the turning point in his career—his second giant step.
He did realize the importance of the work offered to him.
However, there were many things to take into consideration,
details known only to people who work closely on rings, and
for hours he mulled over figures. Doing the complete job was,
for the young engraver, taking a giant step.

"I called the jobber," Peterson continues, "and quoted him
a price. He said that it was more than he had been paying.

My heart sank, but then he added that he liked our work so well that he would pay the premium price.

"From that point on we did quite a bit of work for that concern. We were making fifty dollars a week. In those days not many workers in the jewelry business were making that kind of money. We worked all kinds of hours, but that didn't mean anything. At least I didn't think so then."

In all his business dealings Henry Peterson has been sincere and honest. For the premium price he received, he saw that the jobber received the finest work possible. There is a ring of sincerity in his voice when he says, "I have never been ashamed to face up to any business dealings I have been in, or to own up to any work I have ever produced."

Following the assembly and engraving work for the jobbing house, Peterson was asked to do the same for a findings house. Findings, in the ring industry, are the parts used in the assembling of a complete ring.

The new customer had seen the work done for the wholesaler and wanted the same craftsmanship in his sample rings. The work had to be done at the findings house. Peterson left his own place for a week, "finishing those samples the way I thought they should be finished.

"When I got through, the owner of the place said, 'How much do I owe you?' Well, I asked for twenty-five cents a ring, he said fifteen cents a ring—and I took it. It had taken me an hour to an hour and a quarter to engrave each of them. I didn't mind it, though, because I knew that he would show those rings to a lot of people on the outside. They would send me work and I would eventually make up for the fifteen cents he paid me. As a matter of fact, I would probably have engraved rings for nothing, just for the sake of having them shown around in the trade.

"Whoever saw those rings wanted to know where they had been engraved. I started to build up a clientele that way. Early in 1936 the jeweler and I outgrew our place. We needed more room. That meant more rent, and I was scared.

"Everyone at home was against my moving. Between listening to them, being scared, and yet knowing that I had to have more room, I spent three weeks of restless days and nights. Finally I made the jump. I moved into larger space at a rent of thirty-seven dollars and fifty cents a month."

Henry Peterson interrupted his story to point to an old, small, dilapidated safe. "See that? It's my good-luck piece. I wouldn't get rid of it for anything. The safe was in that office and I bought it for five dollars.

"We soon needed more jewelers to do the assembly work for my customers. I was doing the engraving on that work, plus other engraving jobs that came in. More and more of it came my way that year. Before long I had two engravers working for me.

"We got busier and busier. By the end of the year we were again crowded for space and had to move again—this time into space that cost seventy-five dollars a month. When I had to make that move, I thought the whole world was toppling over on me!"

The unemployed youngster who had been frightened by a bench rental of ten dollars a month had come a long way. He had men doing assembly work, two men engraving—and a monthly rental seven and a half times his original bill. Not many dollars by today's standards, but today's standards were unheard of in the mid-thirties.

Peterson was growing in confidence as his business grew. Experience was being heaped on top of his engraving talent and will power. He was learning his way around in the business world and being recognized as an artisan of rare ability and business acumen. It was fortunate that his self-confidence was expanding, for the real proof of recognition came as a blow below the belt.

"We got word that the very people who were sending us

work and recommending us to their customers decided I was doing too well in business. They were going to open up shops of their own. Those were hard days. If a man found a way to make a few dollars, it didn't matter how hard he worked for them, somebody was out to 'get' him.

"I had to take bold steps. I thought I might lose what I had. But at least I had reached a stage where I was confident that I could do something if I wanted to. So I decided that while they were building their factories, I would build one of my own to make a ring from beginning to end."

Peterson attempted to manufacture through a partnership with one of his New Jersey friends. Adding the traveling to his long work hours proved more than even he could endure. "I was dead beat!" he says.

Despite the "impossible" conditions of attempting to work during the day in New York and at night in New Jersey, Henry Peterson and his partner managed to produce a sample line of rings before their arrangement was discontinued. Almost immediately the rings were successful. Wholesalers saw and ordered. The jobber who had been so important in Peterson's first step toward success again came into the picture. With confidence in the engraver-turned-manufacturer, he offered suggestions for ring designs and placed substantial orders.

It was Henry Peterson's third giant step. To make the rings, he required more space. It was at this point, in 1937, that his earlier prophecy came true. The agent was unable to give his tenant the room he needed, and Peterson moved his young company. It meant nearly doubling his rent and increased his floor space to a thousand square feet. "A hundred and thirty-five dollars a week," he recalls. "I felt as though I were building the Empire State."

The greatest single advance Peterson introduced was the casting of parts usually manufactured by stamping. Work from the findings houses was diminishing. Did it worry him? On the contrary, it was Peterson himself who told the finding houses that they would have to take their assembly work elsewhere. His own manufacturing plant required the full-time services of his jewelers and engravers. At that point twenty people were working for him. For the jewelry field, he was "big business"—and he was just beginning to realize his potential.

To the person looking for the germ of success it is interesting to note that then, as in the future, Peterson was a perfectionist. It was a trait that led customers back and back again to him. It is a trait that examines every detail of a product with a critical eye. Examine a wedding or engagement ring and you will find it is a complex job of casting, die stamping, assembling, engraving, finishing, and setting. The round part, or shank, is cast through the age-old lost-wax process. In the Feature Rings manufactured today by Peterson's firm, extra gold is stamped into the circular shank at the point of greatest wear. Side pieces are stamped out by expensive dies. Critical handwork (today augmented by electronic machines) is required to solder the stamped pieces to the shank. Hand engraving sharpens the design. There are numerous cleaning and inspection steps. The perfectionist trait in Henry Peterson has led to the use of sonic waves for cleaning rings at one stage of manufacture. This use has led to better production methods. It has explored designs, methods, and new ways to merchandise a product that is ages old. Add perfectionist to your list when you look for the characteristics in Henry Peterson that led to success.

In the space of five years Henry Peterson rose from a state of penniless unemployment to being the head of a recognized manufacturing Operation Success.

The Feature Ring Company performed valuable war work. The engravers and assemblers were suddenly needed for their skills and ability to handle minute parts with precision.

Following World War II, the company spurted ahead.

Peterson sank practically every cent he owned into an expansion and modernizing program. While his staff was on vacation, the entire plant was renovated. In the space of two weeks the plant was changed, streamlined, brought up to date.

Business boomed ahead, but improvement remained the goal. In 1948 that drive expressed itself in the development of an interlocking device that revolutionized the industry. The Feature Lock is a simple device that holds the engagement and wedding ring in perfect alignment so that the diamonds are in full view always. Simple, yes, but so important that it was heralded in trade and national magazines and in jewelers' windows the country over.

Seven years later President Peterson invented the gem-on-gem setting, which makes the principal diamond in a ring appear considerably larger and more brilliant than it actually is. Gem-on-gem settings boosted diamond-ring sales generally. It is a realization of Peterson's saying, "Whatever I have done I have always wanted to be the best."

Today the man who worked around the clock for years has cut down to an average work week of forty hours and looks forward to the day when he can cut down even further. Still under fifty, he says, "I have worked as hard as any man of eighty-five. I want semiretirement. If my business is to perpetuate itself, it must get started in that direction while I am still able to offer help. Yes, my son is in the business, but if he is to attain a position of responsibility, he must work up to it. The business will go to those who have worked hardest and most intelligently for it."

The sincerity of that statement can be measured against Feature Ring's ten-year-old policy of promoting from within. Top men get there by climbing the ladder inside the company. The company's growth record since that policy was put into effect leaves no doubt in Henry Peterson's mind of its value. The promotion policy is perhaps an expression of his philosophy that a man who has achieved material success "must give back much of what he has been blessed with"—a philosophy which keeps him active in several national charities.

"I doubt that I would do it over again," he says. "It took a great deal out of me physically and emotionally. I sacrificed my precious younger years and I've paid the penalty. I should have settled for the happy medium."

Success is not without its price.

The perfectionist in Henry Peterson is still visible as he applies a jeweler's loupe to his eye and examines a new design. An exacting employer—yes, but never so exacting as he has been of himself all his life. Knowing the struggle for survival, he has made great contributions to labor relations in the jewelry industry. He has written or passed on every important union contract of the past two decades. There has never been a strike in his own plant, where scientific lighting, complete air-conditioning, and piped-in music have been installed at his own volition.

Ambition and honesty, aggressiveness and sincerity, perfectionism and tolerance—these are the ingredient characteristics of Henry Peterson. They have raised him from zero, the shape of a ring, to king of the ring industry in America.

17. SPLITTING SECONDS

Charles H. Fetter of American Time Products

IF THE CHAPTERS OF THIS BOOK POINT TO ANY CONCLUSION concerning personal success, it is that the roads leading to attainment are many and varied.

The engineer who goes to work for a giant corporation probably figures that the rest of his life will be that of an important, even though anonymous, wheel in a huge machine. And that might very well have been the destiny of Charles H. Fetter (who refuses to tell what the H. stands for), president of New York's American Time Products, Inc.

Young Fetter had an inventive turn of mind, but this is not the story of a child genius. A true genius would have seen the value of his teen-age invention and persevered, but because his high-school manual-training teacher pooh-poohed the idea of an electric shaver, Charles got no further than drilling a piece of iron for the armature. "I am still amazed," says Fetter, "at the teacher not having the vision to recognize the possibilities of the general idea from a patent standpoint. He might have done his future teaching from his private yacht, as the basic principles of the gadget had a family resemblance to the forerunners of the electric shavers of today."

That remark points up one of the principal differences between the Success and the Also Ran—the vision to grasp an idea and do something with it. But there were other things to do in Trenton, New Jersey, than moon about an invention that was twenty-five years ahead of its time. There were a couple more years in high school and postgraduate courses to be taken there.

Charles Fetter had to have his nose broken in a football game by a future All-American and try to blow up the chem lab. And the postgraduate courses may have served a secondary purpose outside the realm of education. School hours were brief that year, and Fetter saw every vaudeville show that played Trenton. As a result, he never attended another vaudeville show anywhere, at any time—perhaps saving him hundreds of hours for other pursuits.

Fetter displayed typical confidence in his college-selection decision. He wanted to attend Penn State. As far as he was concerned, it was the *only* college. So he shipped his chemistry and physics notebooks to Penn State, then sat down with his father to discuss whether or not there was enough money in the family treasury to see him through his freshman year. With a sharp pencil and a mind to match it, his father allowed that, if Charlie worked during his vacations, it could be done. "Now contact some colleges and decide on the one you prefer," said the elder Fetter, not realizing, of course, that his determined offspring had long since cast the die.

This is the point at which the old-line sort of success story would toss in an array of pontifical phrases. There could be a phrase such as this: "Undaunted by the proximity of the bottom of the family fortune to the top of the family fortune, Charles H. Fetter matched his hard-working summers with equally hard-working college semesters, displaying his energy and mental prowess on the track, the college newspaper, and the school's humorous newspaper as well as in his classes."

Don't you suppose, however, that young Charlie went out for track and the other extracurricular work mainly because he was interested in those particular things? Sure he did. He was a normal American boy growing up in pre-World War I America. Money may have been scarce, but the great panics of '21 and '29 were far in the future. Great advances were to be made in his chosen field, but he chose to spend his time in track training rather than wearing out his eyes, miraculously spared in the high-school chemistry-lab explosion, in advancing his engineering and physics studies.

There is no way of evaluating the importance of his track work to his later success, but it could be that his interest in Penn State's track team did have a direct bearing on later interests that led, eventually, to the invention of the world-famous Watch Master and the establishment of American Time Products, Inc.

Yes, the roads to success are many and varied. There is the straight road that starts with a boyhood interest pointing like an adamant arrow to the goal. That is the easy story to tell. In it the principal character is as clear cut as Greek sculpture. Everything he does, in his studies or his pastime hours, is directed toward that single goal. When such a person is held up as an example of the true road to success, it is encouraging to remember that young Albert Einstein was the despair of his arithmetic teacher.

Charles Fetter kept his eye on many balls, rather than on a single one in the manner of the storybook success. His natural bent toward physics, chemistry, and engineering was of prime importance to his future career, but a young man working his way through college passes many crossroads in four years. A different turn at any one of them—and this would be a different story.

The college student had his own ideas about efficiency and his personal worth. He was not noisy or egotistical on the subjects, but when it came to a showdown, he was firm. Here is the example:

Between his sophomore and junior years Fetter worked for an electric company. He needed the job. There is no doubt about that. If he did not earn the following year's tuition, he would not return to school. It was a job of questionable importance, similar to thousands of jobs held by college students.

The matter of efficiency and personal worth came up when Charles spent a nickel for carfare rather than spend an hour of company time to walk several miles. Charlie put in a petty cash slip for the five cents. The company balked. "They thought it cheaper for me to walk those several miles," he says, "than to reimburse me five cents for carfare. Well, maybe at my salary they were right, but it didn't sound efficient to me, so I got a job in a machine shop."

The goal was money, rather than steppingstones in a direct route to the presidency of his own company. Nevertheless, the following summer's job turned out to be just such a stepping-stone. Fetter went to work for that section of the Western Electric Company which is now the Bell Telephone Laboratories. Those were exciting days for a student engineer, exciting because the field of electrically powered communication stood on a succession of thresholds. It was exciting because he could work in a number of different departments and see developments a-borning. And—in case this begins to sound like the straight-line-to-success sort of story—some of the excitement was owing to the fact that Charlie was able to build "a little resistance gadget which I could hook up with my fraternity house telephone to give me a private phone in my own room when I returned to college.... It was an 'exclusive' that distinguished me as a senior."

After the hullabaloo of graduation died down, young Fetter remembered that the Bell Laboratories had invited him to rejoin their working force—at twelve dollars a week. It was fair starting pay at that time, just prior to World War I, but the president-to-be decided that his summer's experience in the labs put him a cut above the other beginners. He demanded fifteen dollars a week—and was more than pleased with himself when his boss immediately agreed to the 25 per cent boost. Then he learned that, since the previous summer, starting pay for all beginners had been increased to fifteen dollars—a piece of knowledge that spilled the wind from his sails for a few days.

But these were days of rapid developments in the fields of telephony, broadcasting (the cat's-whisker sets for home use had not yet been developed) sound reproduction, and transmission. Subscribers stayed away from their telephones during electrical storms; doughboys and their sweethearts sang, "Hello, Central, Give Me Heaven." Fetter was in on the ground floor of the electrical and electronic ages.

The doughboys were volunteering, and as Fetter and his coworkers wondered whether they should sign up together for the Army, their employers persuaded them that they could do more important work by staying on their jobs at home. Stay they did, to work with the wonders of two-way radios, secret signaling devices, submarine detectors—forerunners by a generation of radar, sonar, and walkie-talkies. Transistors were not even known in the laboratory. Lee De Forest's vacuum tube was just beginning to be recognized for its worth. An amplifier —which today could be contained in a matchbox—was a tremendous, complex affair weighing fifty to sixty pounds, housed in a wrought-iron shielding.

Fetter's straight-line-to-success story breaks down again with the signing of the Armistice. War work came to an abrupt halt. Commercial work was, of course, nonexistent. There was nothing to do for weeks on end but read newspapers and magazines. For a young engineer who had been highballing through the field of electronic experimentation for a year and a half, life was flat.

A coal-mining company in Pennsylvania had a scientifically minded graduate engineer for its general manager. At this doldrum point in Fetter's career the manager offered him a job. The dampened fires of his enthusiasm came to life, and he threw himself into the development work that would lead to greater operating efficiency in the mine. Unfortunately for both general manager and assistant, the former fell ill and had to retire. The company again came under the management of old-line superintendents who failed to see the connection between development laboratory and the black column in the ledger. For the second time in his life—and again on the basis of personal worth—Charles Fetter was fired.

The American economy was moving in low gear in the early twenties. Jobs were scarce. Fetter had $900 and a lot of enthusiasm. With that combination it was both natural and reasonable that he should be one of thousands who entered the business of selling gasoline savers. These were small but impressive-looking gadgets that were supposed to reduce gasoline consumption up to 50 per cent. Though widely touted, they were of such dubious value that they led to one of the day's more popular vaudeville bits. The five-a-day comedian would tell of attaching a gasoline saver to his car that gave him another six miles to the gallon, a second that increased mileage 50 per cent, a third that reduced gas consumption by 70 per cent, a fourth that reduced it 33⅓ per cent. "Now," he would explain, "my only trouble is that every ten miles I have to stop my car and drain five gallons of gas out of the tank." But Charlie Fetter never heard that story across the footlights. Not only had his post-grad high-school days in Trenton given him a lifetime supply of vaudeville, but he was too busy selling the little wonders—"keeping myself going and getting my capital back" —to take time out for entertainment.

He turned to selling vacuum cleaners after the gas savers were gone. Electric sweepers were still something of a prized rarity; Christmas was just around the corner; Fetter made more money than ever before in his life. It appeared as though he had found the highway to good living and easy success. But Christmas passed, and the broad highway turned into a rutted path. The star salesman found that he had been merely a meteorite. His earnings sank close to the vanishing point.

Charlie Fetter had passed many crossroads. Now, he felt, his life was at a main intersection. He was old enough to give his future some consideration, rather than just let the winds of fortune carry him willy-nilly to his next job.

Fetter's "one-man conference," at which his future was the only business on the agenda, was apparently conducted along sensible lines. A less realistic person, looking back at the easy money that came from selling vacuum cleaners, would have chosen differently. It would not have been difficult to have deluded himself with the belief that he was *intended* to sell, that a new horizon was just around the corner, that he was to be a Diamond Jim Brady. But Charles H. Fetter remembered his own name, and failed to see the nickname "Diamond" in front of it. His background, experience, and personal liking pointed—the adamant arrow at last—to the communications field.

"I couldn't bring myself to crawl back to Western Electric, even though their employment application at that time carried space for 'date of re-employment.' I didn't know in exactly what part of the communications field I wanted to work—or where I might be accepted, for that matter.

"I knew one man in the New York Telephone Company, and I went to him with my problem. That was a fortunate step for me, as it happened that he was a good friend of Lloyd Espenshield of the American Telephone and Telegraph Company, who was one of the early research workers in radio and wired telephony. My friend in New York Tel arranged an interview with Mr. Espenshield. As a result, I was taken into the research department of A. T. and T.

"Perhaps this is the place to say that from that time in 1919 until 1937, when I formed American Time Products, there was not a single assignment in my experience which was not connected in some way with new ideas and new subjects in this ever-changing field of communications. It held my interest and my work at the peak at all times."

Lucky C. H. Fetter! Even if he had never become president of his own company, the importance of his one-man conference is obvious. Few men can have their interest held at its peak by their job for nearly twenty years.

Fetter worked on one of the problems bothering A. T. and T. in 1919—a problem that gave him firsthand knowledge of the back yards of Brooklyn, then whisked him to country areas of northern New Jersey. Subscribers had lost some of their fear of using a telephone during an electrical storm, but they hesitated to use it for personal matters. Incredible as it may sound today, telephone conversations in some areas poured out of neighbors' loud-speakers. "I found," says Charlie Fetter, "that in 99 per cent of the cases the sounds that were overheard were complex jumbles of several voices, and only occasionally was it possible to overhear intelligible speech. The matter was of grave concern to all of the officials at A. T. and T., because the safeguarding of telephone conversation secrecy is one of the first considerations in a voice-communications system."

The problem was licked after being traced to an oscillating antenna circuit. More modern design, eliminating that circuit, wiped out the electronic eavesdroppers. Next, Fetter was one of the men who worked on station WBAY, A. T. and T.'s New York radio station. It was to operate on 400 meters, in competition with WJZ's 360 meters. There was just one hitch. WBAY worked least efficiently on 400 meters and gave its best signal on 360 meters.

Before the silent antenna was scrapped, Fetter was working on his next assignment. He was one of the instructors who taught radio-station personnel radio-operating technique. He grappled with the problem of relaying remote programs to the radio transmitter, developed the so-called shunt type of equalizer which makes it possible for telephone cables to carry high frequencies as well as low and which is still used for that purpose. He worked on "wire broadcasting" systems. Dozens of different types were tried, including a successful trial installation of broadcasting over power circuits, as opposed to communication circuits. Some of the ideas led to the technical success of "piped" music for restaurants and hotels.

Loud-speakers changed from horn type to cone type. Fetter was one of the group first to demonstrate this advance to officials of A. T. and T. He worked on the telephone circuit that ran from New York City to Rocky Point, Long Island, installing his equalizers along the line so that the signal would be strong enough when it reached Rocky Point to hop the Atlantic to London. The circuit worked, and for the first time man's voice bridged the ocean as a forerunner of two-way transoceanic telephony.

The business of voice transmission, by wire and radio, was a growing giant, and giants are not without their dangerous moments. Telephone linemen were occasionally killed by a sudden leap in voltage in the lines. Charlie Fetter was one of the company's flying squad that scoured the country for danger points. The hazard came from improperly designed power lines, such as overhead lines for electric railroads.

As in any sort of prosecution, it is one thing to locate a culprit, but quite another to prove that he is a culprit. Fetter and his coworkers built special recording devices that photographed any disturbance in the telephone lines and simultaneously photographed a clock to show just when the renegade electricity leaped from the power line.

Just about the time the pioneering atmosphere of that work began to wear thin, Charles Fetter was transferred to Electrical Research Products, Inc., the Bell System company that worked with motion-picture studios. The movies were just learning to talk, and technical instructors were needed.

Fetter worked on newsreel trucks and their big brothers, the location trucks, which were more complex. He recorded the famous MGM trademark, a roaring lion, at a zoo in 1922. For Paramount, he took his recording equipment into an airplane and made about a dozen dives to within a hundred feet of the ground—an experience that caused him to keep his feet on the ground for some years. (The sound track was never used.)

With feet firmly on the ground, Fetter worked on new ways to record for motion pictures, ever seeking greater fidelity, and following one new development with another. Returning to New York in 1929, he became involved in a transatlantic mixup which became one of the reasons for establishing his own company. Charlie Fetter volunteered to go to Italy "for two months, to teach someone over there how to operate a location truck." Somehow he wound up in England, and the two months became two years, during which he helped establish sound-recording systems in British studios.

"On my return," says Fetter, "I felt like a man without a country. Many of my old pals had been shifted and the work took on a different complexion. Without any definite assignment, I puttered around with precision timing. I knew that in the field of athletics the closest measurement of time then available for timing a race was 1/10 second. A little arithmetic told me that in a hundred-yard dash, a runner could cover about a yard in that space of time. As you know, races are often won by inches. The time error could be considerable."

This was Charles Fetter's important threshold. The youngster who could not sit still and merely read newspapers and magazines after World War I became the man who must devote his unassigned time to a specific project. Here is the story in his own words:

"Thinking about this matter of timing led me to work on a device for 1/100th-second timing. At the same time, I helped develop a photofinish mechanism. Together these devices provided a basis for both judging and timing races with greater dependability and accuracy. The equipment was used for the first time at the Olympic Games in Los Angeles in 1932. Later it was used at the National Air Races in Cleveland.

"The success of that venture and the equipment that came

out of it inspired the idea of an electronic means for timing watches." Thus in one laconic sentence Charles Fetter sums up the jump that launched him from a past career as an employee of one of our more substantial industrial giants to the questionable prospects of self-employment.

Some of the shakiness was starched out of his future prospects when his first watch timer was exhibited at 1935's National Jewelers' Show. His invention printed a record of watch beats on calibrated paper in such a way that the twenty-four-hour rate of the watch could be read instantly after a fifteen-second test. It stole the show. Today Charlie Fetter's "Watch Master" continues to hold first place in its field, being sold in greater quantities than all other watch timers combined.

An elderly watch repairman says, "At first I couldn't believe it. Ever since I was apprenticed in the trade as a little kid, there were certain things you did, and just certain ways you did them. My father showed me what his father had shown him. It was more an art than a trade. It took years to become any good at it, and always it took at least two days to get acquainted with a watch and discover what was the right adjustment or what should be replaced. Now, all of a sudden, a little machine tells everything about a watch in less than a minute. That Watch Master is a wonderful thing. I wouldn't be without it. But do you know the day I saw it in 1935 I thought my world was coming to an end."

Needless to say, the world did not end for that Old World craftsman or his peers. Rather, a new world was opened for them—a world of *electronic* timing which was so accurate that during World War II Watch Master frequency standards were used by the armed forces in a variety of applications. They were integrated with instruments for bomb sights, weather forecasting, timing airplane speed from the ground, artillery gunfire analysis. Watch Master enlisted in every branch of the service.

Following the war, it found its rightful niche in many fields —navigation, to measure viscosity, fluid flow, chemical reaction, in facsimile work, radiation counting, and speed control. The timing mechanism that is right within limits of 1 part in 100,000 has come of age.

18. BEAUTY ROUND THE CLOCK

Larry Mathews of Beauty City

A FEW MINUTES BEFORE TEN O'CLOCK ONE NIGHT, AN ATTRACTIVE but slightly harassed-looking blonde walked up to the information clerk in New York's Great Northern Hotel. "Where," she asked with a desperate tone in her voice, "can I get a cocktail washed out of my hair?"

In any other hotel in the country, even the suavest clerk would probably have been nonplused by the question. The young man behind the Great Northern's desk laconically pointed toward the west end of the lobby, "Over there, Miss. Larry Mathews."

In this unorthodox fashion another customer was directed to the unusual twenty-four-hours-a-day beauty salon owned and operated by a former photographer, former Air Corps mechanic. Today Larry is recognized as more than a leading hair stylist. On days when he does not appear personally on television, he is a behind-the-scenes consultant. He is a consultant to Broadway and night-club shows, caters to a clientele that reads like "Who's Who on Broadway," sells a special line of his own cosmetics. Today Larry operates not one, but two all-day, all-night beauty salons in New York, a third on the Borscht Circuit in South Falsburg, in the Catskill Mountains; on September 15, 1956, Larry opened his fourth salon at—of all unlikely sounding places—West Point Military Academy.

The beauty-salon business is highly competitive. It is run on a slim profit margin. Less than 5 per cent of America's women comprise the regular clientele. The future for an operator—

operators are well tipped—is simpler and less risky than the future prospects for an owner. Then how does a man, a man who would look more at home in heavy industry or industrial sales, hurdle from photography to success in the business of beauty?

Basically, the answer is a combination of an abiding idea and sheer chance.

Mathews started working as a photographer's assistant ("I carried the camera!") at the age of fourteen. Naturally, he became a photographer. For several years before opening his own studio, Larry worked for a portrait house that found its business by means of the "completing our files" routine.

"It was unorthodox," Larry admits, "but we gave everybody as good pictures as they could get anywhere, and for less money. We would find out who was staying in the best hotel suites in the city, and what cities they came from. Then we'd call and tell the people from Chicago that we were 'completing our Chicago files,' and ask them to sit for a portrait.

"The pictures had to be good, because nobody had to buy them. It's a good thing for me that it wasn't so much of a racket as it sounds, because in my beauty salon I meet a lot of the celebrities whom I had photographed.

"Actually, the only unorthodox part of the whole business was the way we got in touch with people. I remember one elderly man from Tulsa. He bought only a few, two or three, portraits of himself. He had snow-white hair, sharp blue eyes, and—well, I guess you'd call his face interesting and kind—the sort who could play a grandfather on Broadway and have everybody believe him even before he opened his mouth.

"He went back to Tulsa with his two or three portraits, and of course I thought that was the end of that. Then, lo and behold, we got a call a week later. It seemed that the old man should never have made the trip East. It was too much for him. He had died just a couple of days after he arrived back home.

"The reason I mentioned the way he looked is that I 'caught' him. Every once in a while you take a photograph that's head and shoulders above most of them, and this was one. Well, the phone call was from his widow. She had been after her late husband for years to have a portrait taken, but he wouldn't go to a studio. He seemed to think it was immodest. She was so happy about the picture I'd taken, she broke down on the telephone. She wanted three dozen prints at any cost to give to children and grandchildren and business associates who thought the old man was the greatest guy who ever lived.

"After that I couldn't believe there was anything at all wrong with our way of getting business. But the most important thing I learned from that business was that you had to have something *different* to draw customers.

"I opened my own studio and did a lot of commercial work for advertising agencies and public-relations firms. Whenever possible, I'd use a location on Madison Avenue itself for background, instead of taking the picture in my studio. I'd do anything to get people to know me. Customers will go to somebody they recognize before they will go to a stranger.

"I fiddled around with tints and unusual effects. I worked like a dog on a blue tint for photographs—it was expensive, too —and then found out that it had been used years and years before.

"But always I was trying to find something new to offer customers. Then, after the war, photographers were a dime a dozen around New York. I was a photographer in the Air Corps after being a mechanic, but most of the photographers I met in uniform were new to the business. That meant that there were surplus photographers all over the place when the war ended.

"About the smartest thing I did at that time was open a small studio in conjunction with a beauty salon. After all, when is a woman at her best? I asked myself that question, and the obvious answer was 'Right after she's had her hair set.' Now I have a photographer at Beauty City (Larry Mathews' theater district salon) and here in the Great Northern Hotel."

Norma, Larry's attractive ash-blond wife, and ten-year-old Barbara are the other members of the Mathews family. Larry met Norma while he was in service in England. She was a member of the WAAF. In the mad competition for dates that took place wherever servicemen outnumbered civilians, you wonder just what elements attract a girl whose startling good looks are matched by calm intelligence. The answer must be that the British WAAF saw something more in Mathews than "just another G.I." Talk to Norma Mathews for three minutes, and you know she could have had her pick and choice of a regiment.

Back in the States as a civilian, Larry became—well, discouraged is probably too strong a word. More precisely, he was unhappy about the prospects of a photographer in a city crowded with photographers. Even his sound basic idea of giving customers something new, something more than they bargained for, was not enough to keep his income up to the level he wanted.

Late one night Norma and Larry were propped up in bed, scanning early editions of the newspapers. Norma was glancing through the help-wanted ads. "You know, Larry," she said, "there must be a lot of money in the beauty business. Just look at all the ads for beauticians."

"Most people outside the business make the same mistake," Larry says today. "They figure that we must be making a lot of money. After all, what do we use? Water. That's cheap. Creams, lotions, hair sets. We can use the dryers over and over. Actually, the cost of materials hardly enters into it. Labor is the big cost, but people forget that. It reduces the profit margin to about 8 per cent, and if I have one bad week, I figure that it takes me seventeen weeks to make up for it."

That, however, was knowledge still hidden from both of the

people adding up the number of "Beauty Operator Wanted" ads that night in their Bronx apartment.

"Let's do it!" said Larry. The next day Norma enrolled in a beauty school and Larry applied for enrollment under the G.I. Bill. After graduation, Norma went to work in the Bronx, then opened her own neighborhood beauty salon while Larry continued to work for others, learning all he could about cutting, styling, coloring, equipment. Finally, Larry was ready to launch his own business.

"I've got the idea," he told his wife one evening. "I'll run a beauty salon all day and all night so that women won't be slaves to beauty-shop hours." Mrs. Mathews agreed that it sounded like a great idea. Larry shopped around for a good location and finally chose the Great Northern Hotel on fashionable West Fifty-seventh Street.

Today, with operators busy around the clock in both New York City locations, Mathews' idea looks like an obvious "natural." It would seem that his basic idea of giving customers something new—in this case releasing them from arbitrary beauty-shop hours—combined with the chance luck of counting up the help-wanted ads, would combine to point directly to success. But where one idea makes an immediate blaze, another must smolder until enough heat is generated to cause the fire to break through. It was that way with the all-night beauty salon.

The idea of being able to have a shampoo, rinse, or permanent at 11 P.M. or 3 A.M. did *not* bring customers in by the expected carloads. Women came, sure—curiosity seekers; women who wondered what kind of women had their hair curled at midnight. They would stand outside the glass doors and ogle at the few customers who patronized Larry's monstrous innovation.

"There weren't enough girls who needed cocktails shampooed out of their hair to keep me in business," Larry says. "Norma and I were almost strangers. She had her neighborhood shop to keep her busy all day, and I had my shop to keep me busy all day and all night. If it hadn't been for that shop of Norma's, I'd have been out of business in a month. Her place kept me going until the idea caught on.

"No, there was no spectacular publicity. I was mentioned here and there in the newspapers, but I don't know whether that publicity brought me customers or just curiosity seekers at first. Little by little the curiosity seekers discovered that *normal* women came to have their hair done at the end of an evening, or when they couldn't sleep.

"Do you know where a lot of my late-hour customers came from in the first year? France! I was written up in a French magazine, and I think every woman who read the magazine and visited New York came to the place to have her hair done in the middle of the night."

One innovation is enough for some people. Larry likes to pile one on top of another. He experimented with hair colorings, traveling through several European countries until he found what he wanted in Paris. It was a product intended to intensify the whiteness of white or faded hair. Through experimentation, Larry used it to produce strong colors for an exotic appearance. (The French manufacturer later claimed the trick colors as his own. By that time Larry Mathews had galloped on to new fields and could not find time to do more than say, "How do you like that!")

Returning to New York, the beautician turned hair colorist demonstrated the coloring to the management of the world-renowned night club, the Copacabana. They liked the idea, and almost immediately the "Copa girls" appeared with orchid hair. The color would never sweep the country as a replacement for blond, but it made Larry a "personality" almost overnight.

Girls from the Copacabana were to be seen almost daily in the Great Northern, on their way to or from Mathews' salon. A more appealing, eye-arresting form of animated advertising would be hard to devise. After several months the orchid hair color became dated, as do all things in night-club revues except

feminine pulchritude. Larry called the girls into his shop one
by one and removed the coloring.

"Well, that's that," he told his wife as one of the willowy
beauties left the beauty salon.

"I don't think so," replied Norma. She rechecked the list of
Copa girls. Sure enough, one girl had not kept her appointment
to have the color removed. Larry telephoned and reminded the
lass.

"But I have naturally orchid hair!" she informed him. Larry
has not yet fully recovered from the shock.

Norma Mathews sold her uptown beauty shop but is far
from escaping the demands of a business that sells "beauty
'round the clock." She spends much of her time backstage at
the Copacabana or in television dressing rooms giving last-
minute touches to coiffeurs and make-up. Daughter Barbara
attends boarding school in Darien, Connecticut, so that both
parents can attend to business—working in relays when necessary—without guilty parental consciences.

Attending to business means, for Larry, working on a schedule that competes with his beauty salons' hours. He appears on
one television show once a week, on another once a month,
and gives daily advice on make-up and hair styling. Even that
does not complete his schedule or fill out Mathews' pattern for
success, the piling of one innovation atop another.

Off and on for three years Larry worked with a chemist to
develop a complete line of unusual cosmetics.

"There are a lot of good cosmetics on the market. They're
made by big companies. I couldn't compete with them," he
says. "Of course I could have bought a line of ready-made
cosmetics with my own label on them, but *anybody* can do
that." The way Larry says it, you know immediately that he
would scratch the idea that *anybody* could use.

"What could I do in cosmetics that was different, that gave
something extra? When I finally looked at the problem that
way, the answer came to me—cosmetics for the 'problem' face.

You know, the girl with an allergy to ordinary creams, the person with acne or scar tissue.

"Maybe you think a woman uses make-up only for vanity. It's not always the case. The girl who is unattractive because her face is blotchy and the woman with an ugly birthmark on her neck or face—they have a problem that's both physical and psychological.

"A person may outgrow her psychological difficulties, and she may not. But even if she does, an ugly blemish can cause her to miss a lot of fun when she's young—dances, parties, all the things that are so darned important just at the age when some poor kids' faces act up and break out."

Thinking about it in that vein, Mathews saw more than just another line of cosmetics. He and his chemist struggled through formula after formula for each preparation until achieving a result that would solve the problem. Oh, yes, the cosmetics work just as well on a clear complexion.

The abiding idea of doing something different, of giving people more for their money whenever possible, had been linked to sheer chance to put Larry and his wife in the beauty business. The abiding idea was teamed with imagination, reason, and reasearch to produce the unusual cosmetics. "I'll never put the big boys out of business," says Larry, "but I'm not trying to."

Another man would grow ulcers forcing his products. Larry relaxes and grows new ideas. A "black light" rinse is one of his newest. Designed, like the orchid dye, for glamorizing entertainers, it changes color under the invisible rays of black light. The startling effect is pure showmanship.

As this is being written legal wheels are turning to patent another Mathews innovation—a home beauty kit women can use to "tip" or "streak" their hair with highlights of ash blond. Except for Larry's new kit, the effect can be had only by visiting a beauty salon.

Twenty-four-hour beauty service was only the starting point

for the second Mathews salon in New York, Beauty City on West Forty-seventh Street. From the enlarged salon on Fifty-seventh Street the idea was carried over to arrange the driers in tiered curves so that women sitting under them could watch the hair stylists at work. "In the Metropolitan," says operatic star Zinka Milanov, "I am in the spotlight. Everybody watches *me*. At Beauty City I am just one of the audience."

A separate section houses a beauty salon for children. Drawings of childhood characters adorn the walls. Lollipops are free. Moppets leave the salon's fairy-tale chairs glowing like a million dollars—at a cost considerably less.

More recently part of Beauty City's 8,000 square feet of floor space has been made into a health club. Showers, steam cabinets, a hot room, massage tables, and masseuses until midnight. After midnight? Another innovation! The health club has the country's first coin-operated vibrating massage tables. "A woman puts in a dollar," says Larry, "and gives herself a two-dollar massage.

"We had the tables made especially for Beauty City. They'll be all over the place in a little while, I suppose. People come down to look at them, because they can't figure out by themselves how a coin-operated massage table works."

Coin-operated dispensers in another section of the salon provide light snacks—coffee, soft drinks, sandwiches. And in addition to the special cosmetics, a woman can purchase a handbag or evening bag, perfume, jewelry, even a dress.

A well-known actress, popular on both sides of the Atlantic, was saved from "disgrace" by the extra services at Beauty City. Her luggage disappeared somewhere between Paris and Idlewild Airport. Considering the extent of her wardrobe and the amount of luggage involved, its disappearance compared with Mark Twain's hoax about the missing white elephant. At least she would be able to have her hair done, even if all of New York's stores were closed. Between the time of her previous visit to Larry's salon in the Great Northern Hotel and that night he had opened Beauty City. The actress selected a dress, jewelry, and an evening bag, leaving the salon in high spirits for her New York reception party.

"She could have gotten by with the clothes she had on," Larry recalls. "I got more of a kick out of the dates we've saved or made possible for the office workers and housewives. A new hair-do and proper make-up can work wonders for a girl, but she can't feel right if she's wearing a business suit."

The accessories and clothes available at Beauty City sound, at first, like a high-priced "come-on." You have to get the feel of Larry Mathews' thinking to understand that he would not give floor space to a counter of overpriced merchandise. He is a down-to-earth person with a down-to-earth understanding of the average person's income. If his personal income is above the national average, he has made it through volume business, a multitude of transactions, and repeat customers. The ulcer-raising pace of the get-rich-quick schemer is not for him.

Women can enjoy frequent hair sets and periodic waving, cutting, and styling at economical prices by joining a Beauty Club. Make-up consultations—including the actual making up of a woman's face—are free. "Women enjoy it," says Larry. "They must. They come back."

What would he do if he ran dry of ideas? "I don't think I ever will. They keep coming. There is always something new to do if you keep your eyes open," says the beautician.

Underneath those laconic words are qualities that help keep the ideas coming. The principal quality is one of relaxation. The man may have worked twice around the clock, but at the end of it he is in a state of relaxed tiredness rather than tense weariness. Another important quality is Larry's ability to see things through imaginative eyes. No dolt could have conceived the theatrical arrangement of his beauty salons, or any of his other innovations.

Stating that relaxation is an important quality in a man who is always busy sounds paradoxical. If it is paradoxical, Larry

Mathews has found the way to mix the two elements. The key is that he refuses to worry.

When home-permanent kits came on the market, backed by heavy sales promotion, beauty-shop operators as a whole were frightened. They saw their livelihood threatened, felt that they were in the position of the iceman when electric refrigerators became popular. Beauticians' associations held emergency meetings. Some ran advertisements to counteract the effect of home-permanent-waving-kit advertising, if they could. Larry looked into the matter calmly, drew his own conclusions, and waited for increased business.

It came. "Many women," he says, "discovered that they could not style their own hair. They could wave it, but a wave without styling doesn't amount to very much. What the home-permanent kit did was make them conscious of beauty treatments."

Look at a problem imaginatively. Do something "different." And stay relaxed. Larry Mathews has combined those attitudes in a beauty-shop Operation Success. They can be adapted in any other field.

19. THE RED SHIELD—
AND COURAGE

The Salvation Army

A CHAPTER ON THE SALVATION ARMY IN A BOOK DEALING WITH business successes? At first glance, it could seem out of place. Consequently, some justification must be given.

For the length of this chapter, assume that Christianity is listed on the Stock Exchange. Assume, further, that you are considering buying some shares under one brand name or another. At this point you want to know how the Salvation Army —a Johnny-come-lately founded in England in 1865—has succeeded in the United States. What has it done with the service it offers, Christianity, that sets it apart from other "brands"? Where is its market? Has it been aggressive in developing that market? Has research led to marketable by-products? Does it have a "growth future"?

Stripped of the sentimental attachment that usually exists between the Salvation Army and its proponents or beneficiaries, the organization becomes a dynamic diagram for the business-man devoted to the success of his company.

William Booth, the Army's founder, entered the ministry of the Methodist New Connexion Church in England in 1852, at the age of twenty-three. Nine years later, he started evangelical work independently in the poor section of London. With the help of his wife, companion, and "business partner" Catherine, William Booth founded the East London Revival Society in

'65. Shortly it became known as the Christian Mission, and the struggling organization adopted its present name in 1878.

The Salvation Army was "exported" to the United States two years later. George S. Railton and seven "lassies" arrived at the Battery in New York City, knelt down to say their first prayers on American soil, then set out with admirable singleness of purpose to "conquer for Christ."

Charles Dickens had only five years to live when William and Catherine Booth began their work in Whitechapel. The days of Dickens's major works were behind him. He had thrown a searchlight on the conditions of the poor. But the power had gone out of his pen. It remained for Booth to march in where Dickens had pointed and Cruikshank had drawn his remarkable illustrations of life among the impoverished, the forgotten, homeless, and—as Booth called them—the "unchurched."

Both England and America were far from the present-day status of charitable, spiritual, and social work that sends trained persons into the slums and prisons to help the unfortunate. Lincoln, whose career was closing as Booth's opened, had said, "God must have loved the poor people, He made so many of them." Few could understand the kindly love and charity of his words then; it had not yet become "fashionable" to inspect the slums. More were inclined to take the words of Christ out of context and quote from the twelfth chapter of John, "The poor always ye have with you." Judging by the disregard for the needy, that was followed by a silent quotation from Isaiah, "Grind the faces of the poor!"

In the same era one of America's most famous clergymen, Henry Ward Beecher, assured his congregation that the poor had asked for their dilemmas, their misfortunes, their station in life, so it was perfectly all right to take them for granted without too much sympathy.

The pervading atmosphere must be appreciated to under-

stand the drastic quality of the step taken by William Booth
when he organized his evangelical group in London's slum section. George Railton, as "export manager" to the United States,
worked against the same atmosphere of mockery and opposition. Established churches, the law, and economic groups were
opposed to the Army. The Salvationists were greeted by a bad
press. The opposition was enough to make a strong man shud-
der, think twice, change his mind. A strong man, yes, but not
a dedicated man.

The Salvationists were to meet jeering mobs, tomatoes,
rocks, clubbings, imprisonment, even death. Devotion to duty
carried them through every crisis with hallelujahs on their lips
and an uncompromising belief in their Christian mission. No
aggressive businessman ever turned the attacks of his competition to profit with more gusto than imprisoned Salvationists
used their trials to tell the public what they were doing.

What were the fundamental differences between organized
churches and the Salvation Army? What marked this group, so
that nearly a century after its beginning it is still a growing,
dynamic organization with the backing—at least in sentiment—
of nearly every ex-G.I. of both world wars?

Probably the greatest single difference between any of the
established churches at that time and the Army was Booth's
realization that a man was not likely to worry about his soul
while he was worried about his stomach. "Build thee more
stately mansions" brings no response from a man who has no
roof over his head. No, the appeal to the masses of poverty-
ridden outcasts had to be made on a level they could understand.

Ten years after Railton landed in New York, William Booth
wrote a book. Henry Morton Stanley, the "discoverer" of Dr.
Livingston, published a book earlier in the year, recounting his
adventures in rescuing Emir Pasha. His colorful *In Darkest
Africa* took England by storm. Booth compounded the storm

by titling his book *In Darkest England, and the Way Out*. The sales manager who dreams of having his product mentioned in a hit song asks for no more than Booth when he gave his book that canny title. He virtually guaranteed making Stanley's wide audience his own, thus setting the Salvation Army story before the reading public of England—and America.

In Darkest England told the reading public how the Salvationists were taking the message of Christianity to the poor; taking it not as a mental exercise in an opulent church, but in practical as well as spiritual form. The same message would have to be repeated thousands of times in the United States before Americans would accept the "new Army of invasion from England." That attitude and mocking criticism of everything from their uniforms to their accents were early stumbling blocks for the first Salvationists on American soil.

Regarding the Army clinically and, for the sake of discussion, as an agency for the promotion of Christianity, early events in America prove George Railton to have been a rare combination of export and sales manager. Before he and the seven lassies had been in America a month one New York newspaper conceded that "they manage to get on the inside track with a good many hardened sinners who would listen to some of our pulpit orators with deaf ears."

Harry Hill, who operated a variety theater, offered the hall to Railton and the others. "It is the most disreputable den in the country. In the worst slum in the city. Go there and your reputation will be lost at once and forever," said a minister who heard of the offer. "Then that's the place for us," replied Railton. The clergyman, and eventually millions, was to learn that the Salvationists could not be frightened off, that their only fear was of becoming "too respectable"—with respectability acting as a curtain between them and the lower masses of the unchurched.

Harry Hill's interest in salvation was negligible, but he knew a good attraction when it appeared. He placarded New York City with posters announcing:

The Salvation Army Will Attack
the Kingdom of the Devil at
Harry Hill's Variety Theatre
on Sunday, March 14, 1880,
commencing at 6:30 P.M. sharp.
After which the panorama of
Uncle Tom's Cabin.
Admission 25 cents.

The variety theater was packed. Harry Hill showed his respect for the Salvationists by not serving liquor while the service was on, but considered them "a set of damned fools" when Railton refused payment for appearing on the stage.

The Army provides food, clothing, shelter, guidance, counsel, and other services for man's immediate needs, but its goal is the salvation of his immortal soul. At every service persons who are "reached" by the Army's message are invited to come to the penitent form, to become converts willing to live for Christ alone.

No one came to the penitent form that Sunday night. The Army's first service might be counted a failure. However, as they were leaving, a disreputable wretch greeted them. He had not had the quarter admission, but he wanted to learn more about the Salvation Army. His name was Jimmy Kemp—"Ash-barrel Jimmy" was his more well-known name, a sobriquet given him by a policeman who had found him burrowing head-first in an ash barrel for his hat during one of his drunken binges.

The next day "Ash-barrel Jimmy" became the first American convert. He led a long, useful life as a soldier and officer in the Salvation Army.

Another outgrowth of the appearance at Harry Hill's theater was publicity. Overnight the city knew just what type of person the Salvationists considered a prospect for redemption, and mission houses opened their doors to the newcomers.

In short order there was not a mission house large enough to hold the crowds that came to see and hear the Salvationists. Seeking to hold outdoor services, as the Army did in England, George Railton went to Mayor Edward Cooper, son of Peter Cooper the philanthropist, and asked permission. The mayor cited an ordinance prohibiting all but licensed clergymen from preaching on the streets.

The following day Railton was once more at City Hall. This time he presented the mayor with a "legal notice"—at least it appeared to be that. It announced that unless permission were granted the Salvation Army to hold street meetings, its headquarters would be moved to a city "where equal privileges are enjoyed by all citizens, ordained or not ordained, in the matter of serving the Lord and saving souls."

The legal notice was good "copy." Every paper in the city ran the announcement. The mayor reviewed his position, and again restrained the Salvation Army from preaching in the streets. Railton replied by announcing that the entire Salvation Army in the United States would pray for the mayor until he allowed services to be held in the streets. Newspapers used the maneuver in news reports, editorials, and cartoons. "Past Praying For" was the caption of one cartoon. Beyond a doubt Railton had the ability to get the name of the Salvation Army before the people, and keep it there.

Railton's newsworthy attempts to sway Mayor Cooper failed. The commissioner left two lassies in New York and moved the Salvation Army's headquarters to Philadelphia, pausing en route to establish a corps in Newark, New Jersey.

Later in the same year, 1880, the Salvationist was in St. Louis, eager to expand the Army's work into the brawling West. A disturbance occurred at the first meeting he held in that city, and after that no one was willing to rent him a hall. Nor would the city fathers permit street services to be held.

What to do in a strange, forbidding city that would not permit even the use of its icy streets? "It struck me," wrote Railton, "that the authorities could have no power over the iced Mississippi, especially on the Illinois side, so after distributing handbills to most of the men hard at work breaking Sunday, cutting and hauling ice, I went over to the part where the skaters were and began to sing. It was quite a novelty to have a congregation come skating around me at a speed that made it seem certain that some would overturn others, but they all seemed too much at home for that, and I spoke plainly to them, urging them to seek pleasures from the Giver of all good and perfect gifts."

"This singular Scot who thought it no hardship to starve for Christ" was given shelter and food by one St. Louisian, a pair of shoes by another—a shoe dealer whom he solicited for help for the poor, never considering his own broken shoes as an indication of poverty.

Other powerful figures succeeded George Scott Railton when General Booth recalled him to England. Major Thomas E. Moore, Major Frank Smith, the general's son, Commander Ballington Booth and his wife Maud, the general's daughter Emma and her husband, Commander Frederick Booth-Tucker, and yet another daughter who was to become the most famous Salvationist in America, Commander Evangeline Booth.

However, even so brief a recapitulation as this of the Salvation Army's successful growth would err if it dealt at length with personalities. No organization can be greater than the people that comprise it and the ideas that motivate them. To members of the Salvation Army, implementing Christian charity is of far greater importance than crediting the individual Salvationist for his work.

In 1882 the Army expanded from four to fourteen corps,

giving an indication of the way in which it was to multiply its
centers in the years ahead. Its particular brand of Christianity
attracted many young people. After a short training period,
many of them went out in pairs to establish new corps.

Two young men, with only a few dollars, would hire a
rundown building in which they could live and hold meetings.
They would patch up and clean the building, have handbills
printed, play martial hymns on street corners, preach, conduct
services, and reach out a helping hand to the needy.

The schedule of the Baltimore Corps, which is typical of
the early days, has been called "a study in human fortitude."
Open-air meetings and hallelujah marches every evening at
seven twenty-five were followed by indoor services at eight.
Wednesday saw soldiers' roll call, Friday a holiness meeting,
Saturday a "hallelujah free-and-easy." Sunday services started
with "knee drill" at 7:00 A.M. There was an open-air meeting
at ten-thirty, a consecration service at eleven. A second open-
air meeting at two-fifteen in the afternoon was followed by
an "experience meeting" at three. A 7:00 P.M. open-air march
preceded a great salvation meeting an hour later. Officers
were also to devote several hours a day in house-to-house visi-
tation, spend an hour a day drill marching, train male members of the corps to play band instruments and the lassies to
beat tambourines. They were also to visit any soldiers absent
from roll call and to instruct new converts. Frequent detailed
reports were also required.

These demands on an officer's time and energy, equaled and
sometimes surpassed today, make it apparent that the Salvation Army was not a career for Sunday Christians. But if the
Army demanded self-reliance and initiative, it developed an
action program which calls upon those faculties. That program
could serve as an adaptable blueprint for organizations with
networks of field offices engaged in less spiritual activities.

When emergencies arise, persons in calamity areas are invariably impressed by the speed with which the Salvation

Army moves in with help. In instance after instance it has been the first organization to offer relief to victims of flood, fire, and windstorm, although little of its effort is devoted to publicizing the fact.

No organization could do that and remain a "personality organization" dependent upon a central figure, or even dependent upon the orders and approval of a central headquarters. On the contrary, each officer becomes acquainted through the *Officer's Handbook* with his responsibilities to give aid and provide relief when disaster strikes either his or a nearby area. Thus, when an emergency arises, the center of disaster becomes a magnet for all surrounding Salvation Army corps.

Whatever vehicles they have or can commandeer are loaded with emergency requirements, from broth to bandages. The aim is to provide help, and the Salvation Army doesn't miss.

The early attacks on the Salvation Army waned rapidly in the East, but not before the soldiers and lassies had proven themselves. There were arrests in Syracuse, Buffalo, Bridgeport, New Haven, Cleveland, Dayton, Wheeling, Brooklyn, Schenectady, Utica. Upon their release, many of the Salvationists were announced as "Hallelujah Jailbirds"—but even in prison they had been at work. Today there are no arrests of Salvationists, but many of them still go "behind bars"—as the trusted visitor, confidant, and helper of first offender and lifer alike.

Saloonkeepers particularly disliked the Army. His early observations had led General Booth to link poverty and crime with alcohol, and as there has never been a valid study to prove him wrong, the Army recommends abstinence. None of its officers or soldier members may drink.

Saloonkeepers before the turn of the century looked to local authorities to keep the Army down. Too often customers were attracted away from the bar by the band music and failed to return. One enterprising barkeeper gave an idler, Andrew Mohrant, fifty cents to break up a Salvation Army meeting. Mohrant set out to earn his half-dollar—and was one of the Army's early converts.

Yes, the men and women in uniform had a "brand" to sell and they knew where to find their market. The fledgling American-based Army spread from coast to coast and from California into Canada. The Salvationists' practical type of Christianity came in many forms to fit the requirements of America's unchurched masses. The question the Army asked —the question it persists in asking—is not "Can we afford it?" or "Do we have the funds and trained personnel?" but "Is there a need?" Not a businesslike approach, as has frequently been pointed out, but if the Army's "product" is faith, what is to prevent the Army from using some of it? A record of continual growth marked only by small and infrequent set-backs should be proof enough for the hardest-headed logician that the faith which the Army talks about to others has proved itself.

Dedicated, believing, and energetic, a multitude of Salvationists have expanded the Army not only geographically, but in its range of services as well.

Salvation Army hospitals and homes care for unwed mothers and their offspring. Salvation Army corps headquarters provide home and work for the indigent, recreation for the elderly in Red Shield Clubs. Preaching total abstinence, the Army nevertheless provides guidance and help for alcoholics. Girls seeking escape from intolerable home life find lodging and job-hunting help. When they advance in the business world, they may find more pleasant surroundings in other dwellings operated by the Salvationists. The Army's foundling homes provide individualized care, rooms, and wardrobes. Social workers counsel moribund families. Doctors who are also Salvation Army officers rank with "civilian" surgeons and medical men. The Army's Missing Persons' Bureau often succeeds where government agencies fail. It is the bureau's policy not to reveal the whereabouts of a "found" person, however, if that person wishes to remain "missing," and will return a report only to the effect that he or she is living and well.

At Eastern Territorial Headquarters in New York is an arresting sketch of the head of Christ. It is the work of a prisoner serving a life term, a man who had stepped beyond the borders of hope before the Army brought its message to him. Today he is a changed man.

Young women in prison frequently confide in a Salvationist when they will not talk to police or legal counselors, or even members of other organizations. Their cares and worries are pathetic. "There's twelve dollars hidden under the paper in my upper-left dresser drawer. Get it and hold it for me." "My other dress is at the cleaner's. Please, please get it and keep it till I get out."

Behind the purely practical work of doing small things for prisoners, taking care of babies, providing meals for the hungry, lodging for the needy, and help for the distressed glows a spiritual light. Many stories have been written in the vein of *Faust* about Satan doing material things for people toward the end that he might capture their souls. The Salvation Army turned the Devil's own device inside out and put it to work for God.

During the tenure of Evangeline Booth, the Army came of age in the United States. Magnetic, attractive, energetic, a finished speaker, Commander Booth reached hundreds of thousands with the true purpose of the Salvation Army. And while she was commander, another event brought thousands of boosters into the widening circle of enthusiasts. The event was World War I.

It was not the Salvation Army's first experience with our armed forces, but it was the first in which Salvationists played a part in any number. They serviced nonprofit canteens "over there" as well as providing spiritual guidance. A soldier without money could always get "jawbone"—credit—and only an insignificant chip of "jawbone" had to be written off as a bad debt.

At one canteen the lassies wondered what they could do to supplement the chocolate bars they had in stock. One suggested that they make doughnuts. Using the top of a baking-powder can to cut out the dough and a camphor-ice tube to punch out the holes, the first doughnuts were made—and the fried cake became the popular symbol of the Salvation Army.

The lassies as well as the men followed American troops so close to the front that they were often in danger from enemy fire and gas attacks. In doing their job in danger, the Salvationists won a reputation and a place in the hearts of hundreds of thousands.

Whether the world has progressed in other than technological lines since William Booth established the London Revival Society in 1865, whether the United States has made other than material advances since Railton and the seven Salvationists landed here in 1880, is a subject that is still open to discussion. When such a discussion includes mention of the Salvation Army, it must be conceded that not *all* the world's advances have been in the realms of science and machines.

The uniformed band of street-corner evangelists in your home town is but one manifestation of an international organization comprised of zealously dedicated persons. In America, the period of mockery, disdain, and martyrdom is over. Still, the attack goes forward. Why? In the words of Norman S. Marshall, incumbent commander of the Eastern Territory, "People are the principal business of the Army, not properties, finance, institutions, or social services as such. God called William Booth to the unchurched. If, then, our principal business is people—unchurched people—we cannot complain of lack of raw material."

General Wilfred Kitching said, in part, when the Army in the United States celebrated its seventy-fifth anniversary, "The challenge of the present is that the spirit of the past should live in us." It is a noble thought, gaining its nobility not from the words that clothe it, but from living reality.

Can faith build success? The Salvation Army is a living affirmative answer. "Wherever there is a need, there is the Salvation Army," expanding by serving, replenishing its own wellhead of faith by giving faith to others.

20. PERSEVERANCE AND PROFIT

Arthur Levey of Skiatron Electronics and Television

THE EVER-SO-CORRECT BRITISH PRESS REFERRED TO THE VISITING president of an American film importing and exporting firm as "a boyish-looking American." Arthur Levey had every right to look boyish. He was eighteen years old at the time. The year was 1922. Arthur Levey had already proved his mettle, but he was to be called upon to prove it over and over again.

Something in him, as a young boy, had revolted against the confining walls of a classroom on days when the ice was solid and safe and slick in Central Park. And after the ice melted and the thawed ground dried, the baseball diamonds in the park again called with a voice he could not deny. Arthur Levey played hooky.

A third visit by the truant officer brought matters to a head. Arthur's father never swore, but his choice of words left no doubt in the boy's mind that he had reached a crossroads— no more truancy or no more home.

"I don't think you should dwell on that part of my life," commented the president of Skiatron Electronics and Television Corporation. "It's not supposed to be the right start in life."

By arbitrary standards he is right, of course, but "accepted" standards of individuals are based on averages, which do not allow for the performance of unusual persons. A dullard who played truant to escape schoolwork would never have succeeded. Arthur, at age thirteen and a quarter years, was fee from being a dullard. He left school, not to escape work, but to go to work. And to do something even more important than that. At an age when most boys are capable of making only minor decisions, he made a major one—a decision that he could stand on his own two feet.

"I had had a weekly allowance of fifty cents, so I had to live as cheaply as I could. Bananas were two for a penny in those days; I lived on bananas for weeks." The man who recalls this had left a comfortable home—his father was a successful real-estate operator—to become a waif in midwinter.

A year too young to secure working papers, young Levey was turned down by one company after another. Finally a department store—hard pressed for someone to trace undelivered packages—accepted him without his "lost" working papers. The pay was five dollars a week, and he could be thankful that the rush of Christmas business accounted for his having a job at all.

With the department store as a reference, Arthur moved from one small job to another. About the time he reached the age of fourteen, he was hired by Loew's, Incorporated, as an office boy.

Levey recalls Marcus Loew, the motion-picture theater magnate as "a gentle, unassuming man." The determined office boy liked the work, applied himself, and in a few months rose to head office boy, with a desk near the front door.

One day he was approached by a gentleman with an undeniably British accent. The Englishman wanted to see Mr. Loew. In the line of duty, Arthur Levey asked what his business was with the president.

"He told me that he was a British film distributor, and he thought it would be a good idea to exchange films with some American companies. He planned to set up import-export headquarters in New York. He thought it only logical that he discuss the matter with Mr. Loew, who was certainly one of the biggest men in the film industry at that time.

"I passed him in, but Mr. Loew's secretary didn't. When Mr. McEnnery—that was his name, James McEnnery—came down again in a few minutes, I knew what had happened. Well, his idea sounded so good to me, I said, 'Why don't you come back at one o'clock? Mr. Loew's secretary will be out to lunch. Mr. Loew just eats a sandwich at his desk. I'll go in and try to get him to see you.'

"Jim came back, but about half an hour late. I had just about gotten him in to see Mr. Loew and come down again, when in walked his secretary. You can guess what happened. She told me I was fired.

"About an hour later the visitor stopped to thank me as he was leaving. When he found that I was finishing out my last week at Loew's—because of what I had done for him—he told me to come to his office on West Forty-second Street the next Monday.

"'How much are you earning?' he asked me. I told him. It was six dollars a week. 'I'll pay you eight,' he said, and of course I went to work for him. I must say that some of the men at Loew's were very kind. They told me that if the new job did not work out, to come back."

It is typical of Arthur Levey when talking about someone else to mention that person's good qualities, to acknowledge a kindness, to repeat his gratitude. This is a trait that schools have not yet found a way to teach or instill.

"Both Jim McEnnery and his wife were kindness itself to me. They had no children of their own, and they treated me like their own child. Every week Mrs. McEnnery would have a new shirt or a tie, even a pair of knickerbockers, for me. Young fellows wore knickers in those days, you know. And then—it was quite an event—Mrs. McEnnery bought me my first pair of long trousers."

Life was not merely a round of presents and pseudo-parental affection. Arthur, working directly under the president of McEnnery Film Import and Export Company, acted in every

phase of the young business. American films were exported
to British distributors. British films were imported and sold to
the highest bidders among American distributors.

As he rose in capacity of performance with the increasing
work of the flourishing young company, Arthur Levey's name
became known on both sides of the Atlantic. He signed much
of the correspondence. Answers from overseas, addressed to
"Arthur Levey, Esq.," came back to the boy in his middle teens.

When Arthur was seventeen, Jim McEnnery met with a
fatal accident. He lingered for days, but doctors were unable
to save him. It was a harsh blow to the youngster who felt a
deep affection for the man who had given him the opportunity to jump from office boy to a position of responsibility.

"I wanted to continue running the business for Mrs. Mc-
Ennery, but do you know what she told me? No, you couldn't
know, you couldn't guess. She said, 'Jim left me well provided
for. You take the company and run it for yourself.' "

There was no gainsaying the widow. "Jim would have
wanted it that way," she said. It was her final word. The company was Arthur Levey's. It was graduation day for the erstwhile office boy; the diploma carried the degree of president.

Using one person as an example does not completely dis-
prove the old adage that you cannot put an old head on young
shoulders—but at age seventeen Arthur Levey did prove that
there were exceptions. However, with the passing of James
McEnnery, a knotty problem arose with American film distributors doing business with the company. Arthur Levey had
to convince these hard-boiled businessmen that the flow of
feature films would continue uninterrupted.

Thereafter, Arthur Levey operated solely in his own name.
The business continued to grow. It handled many of the films
made by independent American producers and imported hundreds of the best British-made feature films.

A little more than a year later Arthur was entrusted with a
heavy responsibility. He was to arrange foreign distribution

for Associated Producers, a company which retained many of
the foremost American film producers, including Thomas H.
Ince, Mack Sennett, Alan Dwan, Maurice Tourneur, and
others. He developed a proposition for the British rights that
amounted to more than two million pounds sterling (nearly
$10,000,000 at the then current rate of exchange), which re-
quired his visiting England. English distributors were startled
by his youth, by the "boyish-looking American" whose stream
of letters and contracts had given them no indication of his age.

Talk to Mr. Levey today and it will take only a short time
to give you an idea of the impact he made on his British business associates. There is dynamic drive in the man. Ask him a
question and the answer will be complete, with reasons. He
will cover the matter from every angle. His answer or opinion
is a detailed report. Another mental quality shows itself at the
same time. Many men, absorbed in propounding a fully-
rounded answer, lose awareness of their surroundings. Concentration blocks their perception of what is happening at the
moment. The president of Skiatron possesses a mind capable of
working on two levels simultaneously. The young president
abroad would have had no trouble allaying the fears of the
British distributors.

He made friends in England. Good friends. Important
friends. He was a business influence on Lord Beaverbrook and
Lord Northcliffe, two of the most influential newspaper pub-
lishers in the English-speaking world. Change, excitement, and
trouble lay ahead, but just then, at eighteen, the world was his
oyster.

The youth matured into a prominent, respected man whose
influence extended from Hollywood to England, Ireland,
Scotland, and Wales. He persuaded the noted British publisher, Lord Northcliffe, to cooperate in the establishment of
the Anglo-American Unity League, to help maintain world
peace. Lord Northcliffe summoned W. G. Faulkner, editor
of the London *Evening News,* with whom Arthur Levey

toured the United States from coast to coast, establishing branches of the League, paying his own personal expenses throughout.

With headquarters in London and Paris, Arthur Levey visited Hollywood, the source of his American films, more frequently. A trip to London, shortly after war commenced in 1939, altered his career.

Oscar Deutsch, founder and operator of the highly success- ful Odeon Theatre circuits in the British Isles and Canada, and also one of the founders, stockholders, and directors with Arthur Levey in Scophony, Ltd., was already showing live events by ultrasonic television projection developed by Sco- phony. Live TV was cast on a twenty-foot-wide screen in one of his London theaters, the 2,000-seat Odeon-Leicester Square. The Monseigneur News Theatre in London also installed the Scophony Ultrasonic TV Projector.

"The picture was bright, clear, and almost indistinguishable from a movie," said the London press. In fact, both theaters successfully showed two or three live television events per week utilizing the Scophony TV projectors for more than eight months, up to the outbreak of war. The year was 1939, when theater television had hardly been heard of in the United States.

TV reporter and critic Phil Corcoran, reporting in the *New Leader* on November 12, 1949, put forth the same thought this way: "Television experts discovered a means of projecting bright and clear images on a TV screen—at a far lower cost to the consumer than he now pays for his present eye-killing set—as long ago as 1939, before television was the commercial and entertainment success it is today."

War burst over Great Britain. Levey was urged by Stanton Griffis, a director of Paramount Pictures Corporation, to establish a company in the United States and continue de- velopment.

The heart of the receiving unit in the ultrasonic system

differs completely from the cathode-ray television tube we are acquainted with in the United States. Instead of a "cathode gun" beaming rays against the inner surface of a picture tube, the receiving and projecting unit in the ultrasonic system is a small cylinder approximately the size of a lead pencil containing a secret-formula liquid with unusual properties and including a piezo electric crystal in the tube's base. Television video waves are converted into liquid vibrations. In turn, the crystal converts the vibrations into a recognizable picture. Two rotating polygons "scan" the picture. The amount of light resulting on the screen is then determined by the power of the light source.

Another unique invention, widely used in radar, the Skiatron tube (from two Greek words meaning "shadow" and "tube"), can be used as either a positive picture for direct viewing, or a negative image for projection onto a large screen. The Skiatron tube is now incorporated in radar installations at La Guardia, Idlewild, National Airport (Washington, D. C.), and many military airports.

In television, Scophony had the only alternate method to that developed in the United States, i.e., an ultrasonic TV projector tube, for the reception of television pictures. From all reports—and the conservative British press was most enthusiastic—it provided clear, sharp, undistorted pictures of very large size when installed in theaters or used in home sets developed by Scophony, giving projected pictures up to two feet wide, and for schools and auditorium use pictures up to six feet wide.

On June 21, 1941, a capacity audience at New York's Rialto Theatre was treated to the initial public exhibit of Skiatron large-screen television. They witnessed the Louis-Cann world championship fight. The broadcasting company objected to having its television transmission picked out of the air and shown in a theater before a paying audience. Legal debates on the finer points of that argument could have dragged on for months. Neither Arthur Levey nor Scophony had the money for court battles. Skiatron large-screen TV folded—almost, as a Broadway critic once said of a bad play, "between the first syllable."

Levey had grown up with the motion-picture industry. He had seen the advent of color and sound. To him, Skiatron in theaters seemed a logical, progressive step for the movie-makers to take. Despite the broadcasting company's objection, the system had proven its merit.

Why, then, has Skiatron not become a part of our movie-theater fare? One reporter said that the story, with Hollywood characters, was as packed with drama and villains as anything Hollywood ever produced.

Arthur Levey finally obtained backing from Paramount Pictures and General Precision Equipment to form an American company known as Scophony Corporation of America. The new corporation's stock was divided between all parties, but there was a clause in the corporate articles that made it possible for the film-company stockholders to veto the suggestions of Arthur Levey, even though he had three of the five directors.

"For a while we waited for something to happen, but nothing did. Poor Dr. Rosenthal, inventor of the Skiatron, almost went out of his mind. He was a brilliant physicist. It nearly drove him crazy, sitting at his desk day after day—no staff, no equipment—working only on paper.

"Paramount and General Precision Equipment had us completely stymied. Without their consent and financial assistance we could do absolutely nothing."

When they originally formed the corporation and signed Levey to a five-year contract, the motion-picture companies' conditions resulted in Levey having to relinquish his interest in film exporting and importing. As a result, the loss of that substantial business left Arthur Levey without a source of income except for a small drawing account—$100 a week—"on account of 10 per cent of the profits."

Bell and Howell, motion-picture-projector manufacturers, offered Scophony $200,000 plus royalties for a license to manufacture ultrasonic home receivers. The offer was refused. Raytheon Manufacturing tried unsuccessfully to obtain a license to produce the Skiatron tube. After that failure, Raytheon asked to buy a share of Scophony Corporation of America. Motion-picture interests in the corporation asked $250,000 plus substantial stock in Raytheon—for a 17 per cent interest in Scophony which had originally cost only $40,000.

Eventually, something had to snap. The wonder is that it was not Levey. As he sat helplessly by, cathode-ray television flourished and prospered. "In electronics," he says, "if you sit by, you're dead!" Skiatron television practically died during those years.

In December 1945, after a thorough investigation, the United States Department of Justice intervened and brought an indictment against Paramount and General Precision Equipment, stating that "An important advance in the TV art had been suppressed." The story was front-paged in newspapers from coast to coast as the first television antitrust suit.

Thurman Arnold, one-time brain truster, James C. Fly, former head of the Federal Communications Commission, and Arthur Garfield Hays, distinguished attorney, were employed by Levey as his legal counsel at different times.

"I was offered a six-figure sum to forget the whole thing," says the president of Skiatron, "but I couldn't do it. I objected to the principle of what they were doing, strangling an invention which constituted an important advance in the TV art.

"One smart lawyer advised me to file a cross-claim against the motion-picture companies. After all, I had given up my film interests because of them. I could show that they had affected my income substantially. And do you know, I was told that the film companies were more frightened by my cross-claim than they were by the government's action against them!"

After nearly five years of battling through the courts, the United States government won a consent decree. Arthur Levey also succeeded on his cross-claim. The film interests, Paramount, and General Precision Equipment, were ordered to divest themselves of their stock in Scophony. In consideration of Levey's cancellation of his cross-claim against them, they transferred to him the stock which they owned in Scophony Corporation of America.

In January 1946, just a month after the United States government brought its antitrust action, Levey had entered into an agreement with a Wall Street firm which undertook, as a joint venture, to find financing up to $1,500,000, and agreed also to provide cash necessary to maintain the company, pending successful completion of the financing program. A nominal sum was loaned to the company, it being understood that repayment could only be made following successful completion of the refinancing program, which, unfortunately, never materialized, leaving Levey in a position where he was obliged personally to maintain the company by substantial cash advances. The failure of the Wall Street firm to complete the refinancing program during a period of approximately three years proved crucial and greatly prejudiced the company's future, because it enabled powerful competitive interests to catch up and outpace the Scophony inventions.

Once more Levey had to look for new—and more responsible—financing. To be sure that his intentions could not be misunderstood, Arthur Levey had his lawyers draw up an unusual prospectus for Skiatron Corporation, which had taken over Scophony Corporation of America, and was seeking an immediate $100,000 capitalization. Levey agreed that any money subscribed should be held in escrow by the corporation's bank until the entire capitalization was realized. If the corporation were not fully capitalized in a given length of time, all money would be returned to the investors without even the deduction of a nominal disbursement fee.

Even before the initial capital was raised, Arthur Levey put money of his own to work. Premises, equipment, and a few engineers were obtained. The company's problems were many, but probably the most important was that the ultrasonic method of television reception and the dark-trace tube had been withering on the vine during the years that cathode-ray-tube-equipped sets were entering virtually every American home.

Skiatron began investigating "special purpose" TV, as well as having its engineers exercise their talents on other electronic projects.

A quality of the Skiatron tube totally different from an ordinary cathode-ray tube is that its surface will hold an image for as long a period of time as the viewer wants to observe it. With a flick of a button, it changes from moving pictures to still photography, in effect. Thus, an airport control tower can "hold" a picture of air traffic at any given moment. Recent models of Radat give a "picture" of air-traffic conditions out to a radius of 250 miles.

Industrial closed-circuit television finds numerous uses for the Skiatron tube. A blueprint exposed to the camera for a second can be "held" for study at the receiving end for the rest of the day, or until the job is finished. A branch bank can compare a signature with records in the main office. As it becomes better understood, further applications are found.

The development of Arthur Levey's career might be expected to end here. He had recaptured his rights to develop and license the Skiatron tube. He had won through to the end of a long and discouraging phase of his career—made longer by the many years of hard work, worry, personal and financial sacrifice, the discouragement and tedium. And—he was no longer eighteen years old. Another man might have considered his career behind him; Levey saw his still in the future.

A significant ray of hope beamed through one important loophole—the only loophole that had existed in the wall around Scophony Corporation of America. The government had licensed leading electronic manufacturers to produce Skiatron tubes, requisitioning the patent under wartime emergency law. As a result, Skiatron was not entirely unknown. Its practical importance in air-traffic control became widely known when the United States ran the dramatic Berlin airlift. In the most closely scheduled continual arrival and departure of airplanes that the world had ever known Skiatron's dark-trace tube was the control towers' eyes. The heavy security regulations that had kept the amazing tube's performance secret were loosened, and the door was open to commercial development, which has now begun to be recognized.

In a company dependent upon electronic engineers for its patents and products, it is fair to ask how a man with Arthur Levey's background fits in. Again we must revert to the phrase "dynamic drive." That is part of the answer. Another part is that when he escaped the bottleneck imposed on Scophony by the film companies, his reaction was the normal reaction of a man suddenly finding himself free from irritating constrictions. Still another part is that his background of association with the Skiatron tube, electronics engineers and physicists, together with inherent intelligence and marketing ability, made the man a "natural" for directing widely different yet interlocking operations of the company. You can judge the man, too, by the company he keeps in his organization—men such as Dr. John Laub, eminent physicist and consultant, and Colonel Frank V. Quigley, formerly on the staff of General "Hap" Arnold.

In 1951 Arthur Levey was still seeking engineers of high caliber. "One day Bill Shanahan walked in, and it was a lucky day for Skiatron," he says, referring to the company's chief engineer.

"I had a job for him to do. I asked him if he could report on a very complicated invention and have the report back in a week. Bill said he would have it back the next day, and he did. It was easy to see that anyone who could grasp a difficult problem that quickly, and had the willingness to work through the night, as he must have done, would be a good man on our staff.

"Bill was twenty-five at the time. Some people would have thought him too young for the job of chief engineer, but certainly *I*, of all people, could not feel that way."

Arthur Levey goes out of his way to pile credit on Bill Shanahan and his engineering associates, including Max Kerman, Vincent Zopf, Richard Duggan, Irving Mayer, and others, for creating and developing Skiatron's unique system of pay-as-you-see television, trademarked in the United States and throughout the world under the name coined by Arthur Levey, "Subscriber-Vision." Whether it will soon be a reality in American homes depends mainly upon the Federal Communications Commission.

The president, chief engineer, and a few other members of the small staff that comprised Skiatron Corporation in the early days made experimental Subscriber-Vision telecasts over WOR-TV's facilities with Federal Communications Commission approval.

Television itself was on its feet and beginning to walk. This was different. Pay-as-you-see television was not yet out of its swaddling clothes in 1949 when Skiatron presented its experimental telecasts, using Bill Shanahan and his associates for more than just engineers.

Both sight and sound in a Subscriber-Vision telecast are "scrambled" at the transmitter by a device small enough to be packed in two carrying cases, simple enough to be installed in about two hours. Subscribers would receive coded electronic cards each month; these cards would have a different code for each program. By inserting the electronic card in a small attachment on a regular television receiver and pressing a simple control, the subscriber would unscramble the picture and sound waves. The punched card would be returned to

Skiatron at the end of each month to determine the amount owed.

Subscriber-Vision is designed to supplement, not supplant, free television. It would make possible the reception of top sporting events, outstanding stage plays, opera straight from the Metropolitan, and first-run movies (even motion pictures produced exclusively for toll TV). It would make available essential and excellent educational programs that free, sponsored television is unable to afford. And, to answer a question that bothers many persons not acquainted with any of the technicalities of pay-as-you-see television, it would not steal any of the existing programs. On the contrary, it would result in additional VHF (Very High Frequency) telecasting stations—including stations capable of using the UHF or Ultra-High Frequencies of the broadcast spectrum. The adoption of Subscriber-Vision would also revive the country's scattering of UHF stations which are economic white elephants at present. A petition is currently before the Federal Communications Commission requesting permission to telecast Subscriber-Vision a maximum of thirty-five hours a week over UHF stations for a period of three years.

A number of medical centers in the New York metropolitan area, with Federal Communications Commission permission, had their television sets equipped with Skiatron's decoding device so they could "catch" experimental medical telecasts. In those early days, Arthur Levey, Bill Shanahan, and a few co-workers would frequently drive out to WOR-TV's telecasting headquarters, then in North Bergen, New Jersey, across the river from New York City. Their extracurricular work supplemented the medical telecasts.

Shanahan would temporarily step out of his chief-engineer role and become a performer. An accomplished marionette manipulator, he was the entertainment mainstay of Subscriber-Vision during its experimental period on the air. Viewers wrote in asking to know why one puppet never said anything. The unvarnished truth is that Bill used one more puppet than he had changes of voice.

Subscriber-Vision telecasts went on the air late in the evening. The performers worked in an unheated garage. The pioneering was as rugged in 1949 as it had been in the early days of radio. Frequently Bill didn't get to bed until half-past four in the morning, but faced up to his day's work at the shop four hours later.

"I don't know how he did it," says Arthur Levey.

"It had to be done," is the engineer's explanation.

Between these two men, as between Arthur Levey and all members of the Skiatron family, there is a bond of friendship that goes beyond the use of first names. As engineers joined the firm one after another, they caught the spark burning inside the president. Like him, they frequently spent three or four nights a week at the plant, wrestling with problems of design and development.

The company's list of patents is impressive. They include a two-way telephone television system; a camera that takes an instantaneous television picture rather than scanning; a microwave generator powerful enough to broadcast in the ultrahigh frequencies; the only subtractive system of color television (similar in principle to Technicolor); and valuable devices in the aeronautic, automotive, and industrial testing fields—as well as Subscriber-Vision.

At this writing larger firms are licensed to manufacture under Skiatron Corporation's patents. In a short time that picture will change. The company, which has been forced to triple its space in only a few short years, is again enlarging—this time with plans to manufacture devices originated by its engineers.

The arrangement now in effect between company and employees is obviously equitable. Through the years when industrial giants have used every possible lure to win new recruits to their engineering staffs, Skiatron has lost only one. He lived a considerable distance from New York City and left Skiatron only because he was offered a job a mere five miles from his home. An enviable record.

Five years ago General Telford Taylor, then special counsel for Skiatron, became chief of the Small Business Administration at Washington, D. C., and introduced Arthur Levey to James M. Landis, former chairman of the Securities Exchange Commission, chief of the Civil Aeronautics Board, and dean of the Harvard Law School. Arthur Levey interested James Landis in Skiatron and subscription television. During the past five years Landis has been acting as special counsel to Skiatron, leading in the fight to get approval by the Federal Communications Commission of toll television.

During 1956, Landis told of the benefits the public will receive from toll television, in testimony before both the United States Senate Committee and the Royal Commission on Broadcasting at Ottawa, Canada. Another supporter of Skiatron since its inception is its general counsel, Kurt Widder, a well-known lawyer in various fields. The Skiatron team is lining up an influential cheering section.

In 1951 all seven members of the Federal Communications Commission, including the chiefs of the Engineering and Legal departments, journeyed from Washington to New York especially to view a demonstration of Skiatron's Subscriber-Vision system. In 1953 the Federal Communications Commission authorized Skiatron to hold a ten-day public test in the city of New York. In the same year, Skiatron was authorized to transmit a special program over WOR-TV, in the New York metropolitan area, under the auspices of the New York Medical Academy. It was pronounced an outstanding success, one which could bring to doctors and surgeons, in their own homes, the latest advances in medicine and surgery.

What is behind this record of loyalty and progress? The answer must be Arthur Levey. One side of his particular genius is evident to even the casual visitor. There is an air of excitement—intensity of purpose, but not pressure. Most of it is directed toward the development of equipment for the government, devices which cannot be mentioned. But one device that will undoubtedly be in for much public mention is Skiatron's Subscriber-Vision system. You may have it in your own home soon. The boy who stood on his own two feet is the man who will probably do it again.

21. PRINCIPLES IN PRACTICE

General Robert Wood Johnson of
Johnson and Johnson

A CITIZEN OF HIGHLAND PARK, NEW JERSEY, CALLED THE mayor of the town one evening some years ago. "My garbage wasn't collected today as it should have been, and I pay my taxes," was the theme of her message to the mayor.

"Where do you live, madam?" he asked. The caller gave her address. A short while later the mayor's station wagon appeared at the taxpayer's home. The elected head of the local government stepped out and lifted her garbage can into the back of the versatile vehicle. Twenty minutes later he was back with the empty can, ringing her doorbell.

"I took your garbage to the dump," he said. "Is there anything else I can do for you?"

If the citizen had had any other requests to make, they were probably driven from her mind by the sight of her "garbage collector" in formal evening attire. She released the mayor from further civic duties for the evening, and Robert Wood Johnson returned to the dinner party he was giving.

You might wonder just what sort of man would or could forget his "position in life" so rapidly. The incident was not a vote-catching gimmick, for Robert Wood Johnson had no political aspirations despite a lifelong interest in matters political and diplomatic. It was not the act of a cringing servant of the people fearing the wrath of every voter in Highland Park. It was the act of a man who has, throughout his successful life, been able to view a problem from the other person's point of view and reach an objective conclusion. This is the rare faculty that led Johnson to propose higher wages when the depression of the thirties was at its worst.

Paradoxical? Not at all. Robert Wood Johnson has certain principles and thought patterns. He sticks to them. Sometimes a result appears to be a paradox—such as a "big" businessman telling his peers that they themselves called the wrath of the New Deal down around their heads. Viewed individually, scanned superficially, certain actions appear paradoxical. Over the long haul, Johnson—General Johnson today—stands out as a remarkably consistent believer in and practitioner of the art of thoughtfulness.

Johnson and Johnson has not grown to be the world's largest manufacturer of surgical dressings and bandages (two major categories in its 1,200 products) by accident. Architecture is one of "R. W.'s" hobbies, and he is an architect in the grand sense as well. Today Johnson and Johnson can point to the General as the man who erected its uniquely decentralized worldwide structure.

Of course Johnson started with a solid foundation laid by his father. The elder Johnson founded the firm in 1885 to make mustard and belladonna plasters. Shortly thereafter he was inspired with a revolutionary idea. In the 1880's, incredible as it sounds today, bandages were made from the unwashed sweepings from the floors of textile mills. Lister had introduced sterilization of surgical instruments as an outgrowth of Pasteur's discoveries, but the world had yet to become electrified to the need and effects of complete sterilization. Why did so many soldiers die in the Civil War? Well, the wounded frequently died. Who could know the answer?

Lister found the answer. He traveled the United States lecturing to interested groups, and one of his most interested listeners at a lecture in Philadelphia was General Johnson's father. He heard. He believed. He decided on a course of action. Johnson and Johnson's famous "Red Cross" bandage was born, the world's first sterile gauze bandage.

Through the years the company on the banks of the Raritan River grew in size and prestige. Slowly it added new products to its line. The industrial picture changed. Products were developed, tested, and approved with increasing rapidity.

One day a new mill hand showed up for work. He was a pleasant young man. His fellow workers liked him well enough to tell him to slow down a little; he didn't have to work *that* hard. They considered it a coincidence that he had the same name as the boss, but then there are a lot of Johnsons in the world.

This particular Johnson was promoted, but there was no grumbling about nepotism among his erstwhile coworkers. He earned the promotion. Through the years ahead he was going to be promoted many times, but he was going to earn each advance.

Robert Wood Johnson is still at home in the factory. And what makes a man "at home" in his factory? The fact that he owns it? No. A man can feel proprietorship toward that which he owns. There has to be a human element to make him "at home" among the machines after he has graduated to the chairmanship of the board.

One business magazine has summed up Johnson and Johnson's policy toward employees—the reason behind General Johnson or any executive feeling "at home" in any of the company's far-flung factories—and the summary is that the company has "a built-in human-relations program that recognizes the obvious fact that since a man's job is more than half his life, management has the responsibility of making that job pleasant, interesting, and satisfying beyond good pay and fringe benefits."

In an economy that divides men into "labor" and "management" and usually thinks of one group as the hero and the other as the villain, any noble-sounding statement of purpose is automatically suspected by champions of the opposing group. Many Americans never outgrow their fondness for "cowboys and Indians." They merely substitute the names "labor and management." Those people won't find a thrill in the amazing industrial relations story of Johnson and Johnson. No one there carries a shootin' iron or a tomahawk to a union-management meeting. Boss Johnson may no longer be a factory hand, but everyone in the labor force knows that he is still working with and for his employees.

When the National Recovery Administration held its textile industry hearings in Washington, Robert Wood Johnson was a "surprise witness." Bandages are textile, and Johnson and Johnson produces them in quantities to wrap up abrasions and wounds by the hundreds of thousands. R. W.'s big surprise was advocating a dollar-an-hour minimum for textile workers —higher than the New Deal itself had dared propose. Johnson's ideas of a man's value and dignity are not limited to articles for business papers and luncheon-club talks. Talk without action is hollow; Johnson's ideas are solid.

You can call the man a pioneer. Our early pioneer in buckskin shirt and coonskin cap was a particular type of individual seeking ways and means of adjustment. His self-reliance was no greater than that required of today's industrial pioneers. When the West was wide open, the trails into unexplored territory were there for anyone to see. The unexplored territory of present-day industry is not so clearly marked. Where would you find a trail?

The pioneer label may be quickly explained by reading of Johnson that "he was born into the business climate of the entrepreneur—the age of industrial giants, the Rockefellers, the Carnegies, the Leland Stanfords—who built and ran their own businesses single-handed.

"But the man who started as a mill hand at New Brunswick and went on to earn the top title at Johnson and Johnson, presides over, rather than runs, the destinies of the company.

He was among the first to see that the 'boss" of the twentieth century can't be an authoritarian. He is himself also a servant, playing a role which parallels, rather than dominates, that of labor, as they seek cooperatively to serve the customer, the community, and their stockholders."

There is a world of difference between labor and management working together and struggling together. At Johnson and Johnson working together covers everything from approaching the union-management meetings with a cooperative spirit to sharing the front entrance.

What happens to profits? How can a man be that democratic without scuttling his business? The fact is that Johnson and Johnson's sales volume is *fifteen times larger* than it was when General Johnson became vice-president and general manager in 1930. After you understand that, all questions about labor taking advantage or workmen forgetting their place become academic hogwash.

The man who could leave a dinner party to dispose of a constituent's garbage, the man who investigated Roman history to learn how to decentralize his organization, the man who can wear a tattered sweater or a homburg with equal aplomb is a complex specimen. He is simple in his in-line, straightforward drive of company policy, but complex in the numerous and widely varied attributes he has brought to his job.

Johnson has the alertness which, perhaps more than any other single characteristic, is the hallmark of success. Some years ago he was a hospital patient. Naturally, considering that hospitals are good Johnson and Johnson customers, he knew a great deal about them. He had been active in their support. He had been a hospital's president. Now he was to observe an institution's routine firsthand, from the inside, around the clock time and again.

What he observed made him sure that a hospital could be run more efficiently, sure that industry's forward strides in efficiency could be put to practical, profitable use by the men and women in white. Trained nurses, although in short supply, were nevertheless handling food trays, wheeling patients to examination rooms, and performing other nonprofessional duties.

Once out of the hospital, Johnson followed the lead given by Harper Hospital in Detroit. He got in touch with his own management people, later with the local chapter of the Society for the Advancement of Management. He advanced the idea that, since health and hospitals were everybody's business, the Society would be doing itself—as well as a great many other people—a favor by giving free help to hospitals. The idea caught fire. Today the Society sponsors an advisory board for hospitals. Its executive director spends all his time working for the board but remains on the Johnson and Johnson pay roll. Hospitals in many parts of the nation far from New Jersey's Raritan Valley have profited through the free use of industrial engineers, public-relations men, personnel directors, cafeteria managers, safety experts, heating engineers, accountants. Today's "beefed up" program grew entirely from one man's alert observation.

On another trip to a hospital—academic this time, not as a patient—R. W. insisted on pushing a wheel-chair patient up a ramp. It could have been a good publicity stunt, but it wasn't. Johnson was simply interested in learning firsthand whether a nurse could push a heavy patient up the incline without strain.

There are other ways to get such information. Measure a nurse's or orderly's pulse and respiration rate before and after pushing a patient up the ramp. A time-study man could be employed. The fatigue factor could be correlated to age, sex, diet, and time of day. It could be developed into a lengthy report with charts and graphs. But years before, General Johnson had discovered that the best way to get something done is simply to do it.

Life at Johnson and Johnson was not always so uncomplicated. The company had grown through the years leading up to 1937. It sprawled out in the United States and spilled over into foreign countries. It had a corps of executives and administrators. A problem concerning an area of responsibility in the production of adhesive dressings came up. It required an executive meeting—and not two or three, not ten or a dozen, but seventeen executives were at the meeting. Johnson's eyes were opened. One of his favorite pastimes is sailing trophy-winning yawls; he knew he would still be trying to win his first trophy if he had that many skippers aboard.

It was at this point in his career that General Johnson re-studied ancient history to learn practical lessons from the methods used to administer the Roman army. He studied the formation and administration of other sprawling economic enterprises, always with an eye for information and methods that could be applied to Johnson and Johnson.

Hand in hand with progressive labor relations, the president and general manager of Johnson and Johnson developed a new brand of executive relations. Instead of keeping the skippers all on one boat, he put each one in charge of his own. The following year, 1939, R. W. became chairman of the board. The parent company became the flagship of the fleet. Each ship was autonomous. If a skipper made a mistake, he learned from it. Junior officers were assigned to different tasks so that each could be tried and tested—not academically, but under actual working conditions—to develop his talents to the full potential.

One "skipper" was sent off to establish factories in Brazil and Argentina. During the next seven years he heard from R. W. twelve times. Six of the letters were to wish him a Merry Christmas.

There are thirty-two independent ships in the Johnson and Johnson fleet, two dozen of them outside the United States. The idea of decentralization has been carried so far that in the New Brunswick plant there is an operations board completely independent of the parent company board. It could be likened to a high command planning strategy on a battleship while the vessel's captain and staff dealt with moment-to-moment tactics and the actual operation of the ship. But no such analogy will cover every phase of Johnson's alert interest in his "fleet."

Through the years he has constantly maintained a broad outlook and kept it coupled to his interest in details. Few men train themselves to combine these two apparently unrelated characteristics. You might find the two combined if you were to visit the company cafeteria in New Brunswick. The cafeteria itself speaks of enlightened management. The majority of the personnel eats there and, by commercial restaurant standards, gets more than it pays for. It is an exemplary way of making the most, for everyone, of the time they spend in factory or office. That's the broad outlook. For interest in details—well, you may spot a man in a business suit mingling with the chefs, cooks, and servers behind the steam table. As a casual visitor it will surprise you more than it does the regular employee to know that the man is General Johnson.

Efficient use of time is an obvious asset in R. W.'s catalogue of characteristics. Without that attribute, the man who heads up the flagship of so vast a fleet would surely find little or no time for other pursuits. But if his interest in practicing politics ceased with his term as mayor of Highland Park, which had been preceded by a year on the Borough Council, it was replaced by other interests and activities. Both before and during his three years as mayor, Johnson served as chairman of the executive committee of New Brunswick's Middlesex General Hospital. He left that post to become president of the hospital. In 1926 Secretary of War Dwight D. Davis gave R. W. a direct commission as a captain in the Surgeon General's Department of the Medical Corps to assist in developing an up-dated procurement program. In 1941 Governor Charles Edison, son of the famous inventor, appointed Johnson as New Jersey State rationing administrator. The following April he resigned to enter the Army. Two years later he was back in quasi-governmental activities. President Roosevelt appointed him vice-chairman of the War Productions Board and chairman of the Smaller War Plants Corporation. And his Army experience was longer than indicated. In 1942 he again joined the Army. In May he was commissioned a colonel in the Ordnance Department, and a year later the eagle was replaced by a star. Johnson was a brigadier general.

The head of Johnson and Johnson has flown and sailed the length of our eastern coast—and then some! Not content with the fair-weather boats that are the pride and joy of most week-end sailors, he has owned a string of seagoing yawls, *Ariel*, *Zodiac*, *Stormy Weather*, *Good News*, and a Danish-built North Sea trawler, *Gerda*. Johnson has cruised to Jamaica. He has made a landfall in Spain, and several times he has sailed north of the 60th parallel, up the coast from New York to Hudson Straits, Greenland, and Labrador.

The latter trips were more than mere exercises in seamanship. General Johnson recalls that "some of this early work was in collaboration with Sir Wilfred and Lady Grenfell, the great pioneering missionaries who served these people so well. We helped carry supplies in the fine Gloucester schooner, *Zodiac*. This was, of course, before the days of radio, when communication with Labrador was confined to an occasional fishing schooner, Sir Wilfred's old hospital steamer, and the annual trip of the Hudson Bay ship."

There were other motives involved in the first trip to Labrador—the lure of gold, the hope of escape from a crowded world, and the vision of unparalleled sport fishing. As R. W. remembers it, "We took along a Mr. Duane Stoneleigh, a mineralogist, in the vague hope that we might find gold or other precious metals. We did find gold—under a layer of a trillion mosquitoes and black flies. Gold is valuable, but for my money, it can stay there!

"Beyond that, my brother Seward and I had the notion that the world was getting crowded and that it would become more so. He and I thought it would be a good idea to acquire a tract of land in Labrador as an 'escape site.' We looked forward to the day of the practical flying boat, and we believed that the natural resources of Labrador might offer great promise.

"Well, we found conditions to be partly up to our expectations, but the bugs took over, *the bugs took over!* There are mosquitoes and more mosquitoes, mixed with a heavy layer of bloodthirsty black flies. Not even a six-pound square-tail brook trout hungering for a trout fly could bring us to try the experiment."

Johnson's traveling was not limited to ground level. Long before single-wing aircraft replaced biplanes, he was flying his own craft. (His plane today is a Learstar, complete with pilot.) He was one of the first to operate an autogiro, an accomplishment he came by so early in the game that the Civil Aeronautics Bureau had not yet devised a standard test for the whirlybirds!

Traveling has taken the head of Johnson and Johnson farther than his seagoing yawls have traveled. As top man of a worldwide corporation, he has left little of the world unseen. Not content with just touching down in a country and seeing the surface attractions, he has studied hospitals in Australia, Canada, China, Egypt, England, France, Germany, and Java as well as in many of the forty-eight states.

Widespread studies of that sort can keep a man busy, but still Johnson found time for other pursuits in addition to his flying and sailing. He counts tennis, swimming, riding, and hunting among his pursuits. He is a Mason, a Legionnaire, a member of two yacht clubs—the New York Yacht Club and the equally famous Seawanhaka Corinthian Yacht Club. He belongs to the Army Ordnance Association, the Racquet and Tennis Club, and a few others. In all, the total does not add up to many memberships for a man in his position. He has other things to do!

In rising to the top post of Johnson and Johnson, the chairman of the board has brought along with him the broad viewpoint. Never neglecting the workingman, he has turned a considerable amount of his attention to the problems besetting management. These are not problems that exist solely in our time without roots. On the contrary, R. W. sees many management-labor difficulties of the present as direct descendants of thoughtlessness, to use a mild term, on the part of the rugged individualist who prospered in the early days. Knowing this historic relationship enabled him to tell businessmen in the days of the New Deal that they themselves had called its wrath down upon them. But knowing about something is not enough for the General. He has taken definite action in numerous related fields to solve labor problems before they had had a chance to arise in his own plants.

Many of us have grown up on stories of the tycoon who pays lip service to industrial relations and works behind the scenes to keep labor in a state of dependent confusion. The theme has provided material for books, films, and Broadway, ranging from G. Myers' *History of the Great American Fortunes* to the happier bit of management baiting, *7½ Cents*, which became the musical comedy *Pajama Game*. Johnson eludes the net simply because he does not belong in it.

Taking his outlook and responsibilities up to the post of chairman with him, General Johnson studied and practiced writing so that he could disseminate his ideas and his company's actions. *But, General Johnson* was his first book. It recounted his Army experiences and became required reading in certain officer-training courses. In the same year, 1944, his first magazine article, "What Business Needs," appeared in the redoubtable *Saturday Evening Post*. Since then he has written no fewer than two dozen articles for magazines ranging from *The Modern Hospital* through *Canadian Business* to *Harvard Business Review*.

Johnson's second book, *Or Forfeit Freedom*, received the Franklin D. Roosevelt Memorial award and was chosen as the best book of 1947 by the American Political Science Association. In it, R. W. kicked the props out from under Adam Smith and his traditionally respected *Wealth of Nations*. Johnson flew in the face of traditional respect to brand old Adam as an opportunist who "voiced long-suppressed resentments, dignified erupting ambitions, fired brilliant but not farseeing followers. Spurred by the Industrial Revolution, they framed a code of business freedom that bordered on nihilism. Freedom, that is, for those who could hold it—and let God pity those who could not!" A man who writes in such a vein is certainly more at home in his own factory than in the pages of Myers' *History*.

Freedom Foundation awarded Johnson its Certificate of Merit in 1949 for "Robert Johnson Talks It Over," the published transcript of a series of lectures delivered to Johnson and Johnson employees. It is typical of the man that the book was *not* titled "General Johnson Talks It Over."

The following year Johnson was one of a committee of seven that compiled a fifty-two-page booklet, *Human Relations in Modern Business*. Into this slender opus went the concentrate of knowledge gleaned from more individuals than the booklet has pages—fifty-three, to be exact. Rabbis, priests, a minister, union leaders, industrialists, and merchants furnished the basic information. If you are looking for a pattern to follow in operating a business successfully, the booklet is "must" reading. It is a more workable key to double-edged success—on the human-relations side as well as in the market place—than can be furnished by efficiency experts or cost accounting. In furthering Johnson's repudiation of Adam Smith and *laissez faire*, the booklet lists five "broad drives that profoundly influence conduct": a sense of dignity, the need for the esteem of others, the basic instinct for survival, the desire for security, and social instincts (the tendency "to associate with others who share their interests and to develop teamwork in pursuing common undertakings"). In principle and practice, Johnson not only discards the old idea of "economic man" and the concept of labor as another commodity in the same general category with coal, electricity, and machinery, he puts them down the socio-economic scale somewhere near cannibalism and head shrinking. *Human Relations in Modern Business* has been translated into many languages and has become a guide for enlightened businessmen and industrialists throughout the free world. It is a Bill of Rights—and Obligations.

Sensing that his obligations did not end within the walls of the Johnson and Johnson empire, Johnson has encouraged employees to take an active part in their local civic affairs. He believes that they should be aware and informed of what is going on in Washington. As a result, the Johnson and Johnson training courses to help a man advance himself in the company have been augmented by lectures on federal taxation and spending. Senators and economics experts have addressed groups comprised entirely of Johnson and Johnson management.

Add up the accomplishments, add up the attributes, and the man who emerges is a startling personality. The paradox of Robert Wood Johnson is that he can balance human beings and a growing, successful business without fear or favor toward either side.